T0318249

Nielsen's Impact on Fathers and Daughters

Daughters Say . . .

"I've stopped seeing him through mom's eyes. I see him now as a man who struggles through life as a husband, a son and a father."

"Things between us were always pretty superficial and awkward—especially if it was just the two of us alone. That's not true anymore."

"Now we're discussing the problems in our family and between us, instead of denying, lying, and pretending the way we've always done."

"We're finally talking about difficult, personal things, including my marital problems and his new wife."

"I understand now why dad and I interact the way we do. That makes it so much easier for me to forgive and to accept him."

Fathers Say . . .

"I was really nervous telling my daughter about ways I've screwed up in my life. But that brought us much closer than we've been since her mom and I separated."

"I dreaded talking to her about 'it'—that one topic that has created problems between us for years. Her reactions were amazing. Why didn't we do this sooner?"

"I learned how to talk to her about financial and boyfriend issues. And she's stopped treating me like a banking machine and a tyrant."

"My daughter finally decided she wants to get to know me. At my age, that's the best gift she could ever give me."

Improving Father-Daughter Relationships

Improving Father-Daughter Relationships: A Guide for Women and Their Dads is essential reading for daughters and their fathers, as well as for their families and for therapists. This friendly, no-nonsense book by father-daughter relationships expert, Dr. Linda Nielsen, offers women and their dads a step-by-step guide to improve their relationships and to understand the impact this will have on their well-being.

Nielsen encourages us to get to the root of problems, instead of dealing with fallout, and helps us resolve the conflicts that commonly strain relationships from late adolescence throughout a daughter's adult years. Showing how we can strengthen bonds by settling issues that divide us, her book explores a range of difficult issues from conflicts over money, to the daughter's lifestyle or sexual orientation, to her parents' divorce and dad's remarriage.

With quizzes and real-life examples to encourage us to examine beliefs that are limiting or complicating the connection between fathers and daughters, this guide helps us feel less isolated and enables us to create more joyful, honest, enriching relationships.

Linda Nielsen, PhD, is a professor of Education at Wake Forest University, Winston-Salem, NC. A member of the faculty for 45 years, she is a nationally recognized expert on father-daughter relationships. Her work has been featured in a PBS documentary and in the media, including the *New York Times, Time, Oprah, The Atlantic*, NPR, PBS and the BBC.

"I predict Nielsen's book will become the standard four-step method for resolving father-daughter problems. Nielsen covers a wide range of issues and her practical, no-nonsense method is applied to dozens of specific problems that no other book addresses."

—**Dr. Warren Farrell,** author of *The Myth of Male Power* and *The Boy Crisis*

"Dr. Nielsen takes her readers, both fathers and daughters, step by step through a process to repair their relationship. The book is at once thorough and accessible. It is both detailed and very readable. It is extremely practical and deeply hopeful. Along the way, each chapter puts a substantial amount of critical research into the hands of fathers and daughters who are desperate for guidance."

—**Patricia L. Papernow,** Ed.D., American Psychological Association Psychologist of the Year, Division of Couples & Family Counseling. Author of *Surviving & Thriving in Stepfamily Relationships*

"Professor Linda Nielsen's newest book is an outstanding work that appeals to a wide audience. Nielsen is the leading authority on father–daughter relationships whose pioneering work commands great respect among her colleagues. She excels in popularizing the implications of social science in an engaging format."

—**Richard A. Warshak,** Ph.D., Past Clinical Professor of Psychiatry, University of Texas Southwestern Medical Center. Author of *Divorce Poison: How to Protect Your Family from Bad-mouthing & Brainwashing*

Improving Father-Daughter Relationships

A Guide for Women
and Their Dads

Linda Nielsen

Routledge
Taylor & Francis Group
NEW YORK AND LONDON

First published 2020
by Routledge
52 Vanderbilt Avenue, New York, NY 10017

and by Routledge
2 Park Square, Milton Park, Abingdon, Oxon, OX14 4RN

Routledge is an imprint of the Taylor & Francis Group, an informa business

© 2020 Taylor & Francis

Library of Congress Cataloging-in-Publication Data
Names: Nielsen, Linda, author.
Title: Improving father-daughter relationships : a guide
    for women and their dads / Linda Nielsen.
Description: New York, NY : Routledge, 2020. | Includes
    bibliographical references and index.
Identifiers: LCCN 2020014244 | ISBN 9780367524289
    (hardcover) | ISBN 9780367524272 (paperback) |
    ISBN 9781003057901 (ebook)
Subjects: LCSH: Fathers and daughters. | Parenting. |
    Communication in families. | Child development.
Classification: LCC HQ755.85 .N52834 2020 |
    DDC 306.874/2—dc23
LC record available at https://lccn.loc.gov/2020014244

ISBN: 978-0-367-52428-9 (hbk)
ISBN: 978-0-367-52427-2 (pbk)
ISBN: 978-1-003-05790-1 (ebk)

Typeset in Bembo
by Apex CoVantage, LLC

Dedicated to my mother, Frances Jean Fandel Nielsen

Contents

Acknowledgments

Many talented people have helped bring this book into being. The enthusiasm and support of my publisher, Helen Pritt, and her editorial assistant, Charlotte Mapp, have been invaluable. And Lea Camarda did an excellent job as copyeditor. I am grateful to these women for their diligence and input. Helen's commitment to this book was extraordinary and deeply appreciated.

Special thanks go to Dr. Warren Farrell, Dr. Patricia Papernow and Dr. Richard Warshak for their encouragement and endorsements. As nationally recognized experts in their fields, they have enhanced my work for many years through their own scholarship.

I am also indebted to the fathers and daughters who have sought my advice over the past 30 years in their quest to strengthen their relationships—and to my many students who have so honestly shared their father stories with me. These are the people who have inspired me to continue writing and teaching about this important, but often ignored, topic.

I have devoted myself to writing about fathers and daughters for more than three decades. Throughout that time my husband, Steve Mizel, has been my most ardent supporter. His insights and advice have enriched all of my writing.

Introduction

"If you do what you've always done, you'll get what you always got."
Mark Twain, 1835–1910

Is This Book for You?

Is this the book for you? You picked it up. You're curious. But why? You might be a father or a daughter who wants to improve your relationship—or who has a specific problem you have not been able to resolve. You might also be a mother, stepmother, grandparent, or boyfriend who knows someone who could use some help improving their father-daughter relationship. Or you might be a professional whose job involves helping fathers and daughters.

Maybe the father-daughter relationship just needs a little tune-up—or maybe it needs a major overhaul. Either way, both father and daughter could be happier and closer. Maybe there are unsettled issues that never seem to go away. Or maybe they are tip-toeing and avoiding any discussions about "it"—that one topic that is holding them back from being more comfortable together. The tension, awkwardness, or distance between them might also stem from the fact that they are making the wrong assumptions about each other. If they got to know one another better, they could narrow the gap between them and sort out their differences more easily. One or both of them might be holding onto grudges from the past. Maybe they're grappling with the same old obstacles that have been hanging over them for years.

For whatever reason, they are struggling with some serious issues or just wanting more from their superficial relationship. What new approaches might help them move forward to create a more joyful, more relaxed, more enriching bond? If this is what you are searching for, then this is the book for you.

Fathers have a profound, lifelong impact on their daughters' well-being—their academic and career success, income and job choices, romantic relationships and marriage, drug and alcohol use, and physical and mental health. Though we tend to overlook this reality, daughters also have a big impact on their fathers. When fathers are not getting along well with their daughters, especially if they are growing apart, fathers are more physically stressed, anxious, unhappy, and depressed. In extreme cases, when they seem to be losing all connection to their daughters, fathers are more likely to become suicidal and more likely to abuse drugs and alcohol. My research book, *Fathers and Daughters: Contemporary Research and Issues*, explains the positive and the negative impact that fathers and daughters have on each other throughout their lives. In the present book, however, the focus is on strengthening the father-daughter bond by settling those issues that divide them.

Why Listen to Me?

You may be asking yourself, "Why should I take advice from this psychology professor? Who is she?" Good question. After earning a Master's Degree in Counseling and a Doctorate in Adolescent and Educational Psychology, I became a professor at Wake Forest University. For the first 20 years of my career, I taught courses and wrote college textbooks on adolescence—the time when father-daughter bonds often become more strained. In the 30 years since then, I have been teaching, writing books, and conducting research on older teenage and adult daughters and their fathers. In fact, for the past three decades, I have been teaching the only college course in the country exclusively devoted to fathers and daughters. I have written five books and dozens of articles on this topic. My work and advice have been featured in such outlets as the *New York Times*, *Washington Post*, *Wall Street Journal*, *USA Today*, *National Public Radio*, *British Broadcasting Company*, *Time*, *Cosmopolitan*, *Woman's Day*, and *Seventeen* magazines, and my *Psychology Today* blog. I also served as a consultant for Mattel toys on their "Dads Play Barbie" commercials and for Procter & Gamble on their Super Bowl "Dad Do's" campaign. As a widely recognized expert on this topic for more than three decades, I am sharing my expertise with you in this book.

Over these past three decades, thousands of fathers and daughters, as well as stepmothers and mothers, have sought my advice about father-daughter relationships. Throughout this book I will be sharing many of their feelings and experiences with you. Reading about their lives can help you feel less isolated and less "abnormal." Their stories will give you the perspective not only of fathers and daughters, but of mothers and stepmothers whose lives are also negatively affected by difficult father-daughter relationships. All of these stories should also give you more courage to tackle some of the problems in your family relationships, since you will be hearing from fathers and daughters who discovered that my advice worked in situations that they felt were hopeless.

What Am I Offering? What Does This Book Offer?

Over time, I have developed a four-step approach to help resolve the kinds of conflicts that commonly strain father-daughter relationships from late adolescence throughout a daughter's adult years. The issues that all too often divide fathers and daughters range from money, to the daughter's lifestyle or sexual orientation, to her parent's divorce and dad's remarriage. Stepmothers and mothers will be especially interested in learning what roles they play in father-daughter conflicts.

If you think fathers and daughters no longer have things to sort out beyond a certain age, think again. There is no "expiration date" for the issues affecting their relationship over a lifetime. Father-daughter issues often extend well into his old age, which is why I have devoted an entire chapter to these late-in-life complications.

I will also share the most recent research with you. "What Do You Think?" quizzes will help you learn about this research in a way that helps you examine some of the beliefs that are limiting or complicating the connection between the two of you. My advice is based on hundreds of research studies in psychology, not just on my personal opinions. You will also be entertained by some fascinating stories about famous daughters and their fathers, including Serena Williams, Lady Gaga, Taylor Swift, and Megan Rapinoe.

The four-step method in this book will enable you to get to the *root* of a problem, instead of just dealing over and over again with the fallout. Discovering the source is far more effective than trying to combat every incident that springs from that source.

Imagine this. Two people are sitting beside a stream. Suddenly, one of them sees a little puppy struggling in the water as the dangerous current carries it swiftly downstream. They jump in and save the puppy. But ten minutes later, they see two more puppies washing down the stream. Again, they jump in and rescue the puppies. But before they can even dry those little puppies off, they see a much larger group of pups in the stream. They start to panic, because there is no way they can save such a large group. The solution, of course, is to head upstream and find out where all those puppies are coming from. In the same way, fathers and daughters need to figure out the source of their difficulties with each other—especially when things seem to be getting worse as time passes.

My four-step method gives both fathers and daughters a set of tools to find solutions to the problems that typically occur at various points throughout their lives together. You will also learn which approaches work best for particular types of issues. Sometimes we have the tools right in front of us, but we choose the wrong one for the task.

Consider this story about travelers who are lost in the desert and dying of thirst. The first thirsty person is lucky enough to find a well. Luck again—she finds a bucket, a rope, and a hammer nearby. But instead of grabbing the bucket, she grabs the hammer and ties it to the rope. She lowers it into the well, pulls the dripping hammer to herself, and tries desperately to lick drops of water from the hammer's head. You can imagine the unhappy outcome. If only she had used that bucket! Like her, you may be using the wrong tools to deal with your father-daughter troubles, even though you have access to the right tools.

The second thirsty person also has the good luck to find a well along with the bucket, rope, and hammer. Fortunately, he knows that he needs to use the bucket, not that stupid hammer, to haul up the water. But there's a catch. Many years ago, he was on his way to get water from a well. Just as he neared the well, he tripped, badly injuring his head on a rock. Dizzy and disoriented, he almost stumbled head-first into the deep well. Worse still, he did not know how to swim at the time. If he had fallen into the well, he would likely have drowned. He is so overwhelmed by his fears from the past that he will not go near any well. So now, held captive by his fear, he just sits near that well, helplessly staring at the bucket and the rope, getting more dangerously dehydrated by the hour.

The third thirsty man is lost in the wilderness with his daughter. Both are terribly dehydrated. They too have the good fortune to find a well. Neither of them is afraid of wells. And they both know that they need to use the bucket and the rope. Unfortunately, neither of them can bend their arms at the elbow. They are able to haul up the water. But neither of them can bend either arm well enough to tip the bucket up to their mouths, and the bucket is too narrow to lean over and sip from. If they had been calm and cooperative, they might have figured out how each can take turns lifting the bucket with his or her unbending arm, hold it near the other person's mouth, and use the other arm to tilt the bucket for their partner to bend forward and drink. Unfortunately their relationship is in such bad shape that they can't even work out a survival plan together.

There are no happy endings in this tale. The point is that the solution is often right in front of us. But we cannot help ourselves because we use the wrong approach or because we are held back by our fears. The aim of this book is to show you the right tools to use when you are thirsting for a solution—and thirsting for a better father-daughter relationship. You will also learn how fathers and daughters can move forward, despite handicaps like the metaphorical unbendable elbows.

This book will help you figure out what changes you could each make to get more out of your relationship. I will also help you figure out what fears are holding you back. What are you afraid might happen if you take steps to narrow the gap between you?

Three Self-Defeating Beliefs

If you are like many fathers and daughters, you may be starting out with certain beliefs that are holding you back. Let me point out three beliefs that will prevent you from getting the most out of this book.

Belief #1: Dad should make the first move to fix this mess because he is older and he is the parent.

Growing older makes most of us wiser in many ways. For example, because he is older and more experienced, a father probably knows a lot more than his daughter does about budgeting money or interviewing for jobs. But that does not necessarily mean he has better communication skills or better ideas for how to sort out the difficulties with his daughter. Besides, why should it matter who goes first? The goal is to make *yourself* happier by finding solutions without getting bogged down in thinking about who should make the first move.

Belief #2: The person who caused the problem should take the initiative—and that person is not me.

Let's leave fathers and daughters aside for a minute. Think back to those times when you have hurt or angered somebody you cared about or loved. It was your fault, and you both know it. In those situations, did you ever feel too ashamed or too embarrassed to reach out and apologize? Did you ever let days or weeks or months go by without discussing what happened? Did you ever feel grateful and relieved when the person you hurt made the first move to set things straight? You get my point: the person who created the mess or did the most damage often has the harder time reaching out, apologizing, or trying to get things back on track. Since people have cut you some slack when you were clearly to blame, why can't you do the same? Again, your goal is to make *yourself* happier by reducing the stress, regardless of who created the difficulty in the first place.

Belief #3: Forgiving someone means forgetting what happened and acting as if it had no impact on me—I can't and won't do that.

Wrong. Forgiving someone does not mean you have to forget what happened. How could you forget? You have a brain that stores memories, with or without your permission. You can't hit "alt-delete" buttons and erase those memories. Forgiving does not mean you have to pretend the other person never hurt or angered you. That would be a lie. And it would require somehow ignoring some powerful feelings.

In the context of this book, what does forgiving mean? It means you stop *punishing* the other person (or yourself) for past mistakes. This kind of punishment can take many forms: distancing yourself emotionally, repeatedly reminding them how they hurt you, badmouthing them to other family members, refusing to answer their messages, shaming yourself for how you screwed up.

Forgiving also means you realize there is a statute of limitations on all crimes. We would not sentence a teenager to life in prison for stealing a car. In the same way, we should not sentence someone to years in emotional prison for their emotional "crimes" against us. Especially if the people who hurt us were not intending to do us harm, showed remorse, or tried to make amends, the punishment should be reasonable and fair—and a pardon or "early parole" might be in order for good behavior as time passes. Forgiving is *not* a gift you give the other person. It is a gift you give yourself—freeing yourself from anger and bitterness in order to get more pleasure from whatever is still there to enjoy with that person. In terms of forgiving yourself, forgiving does not mean believing, "My bad behavior was OK." It means finding compassion for yourself: "I didn't know then how to handle this better." "I was too frightened and insecure to take the right path." Forgiving means grieving for what you or the other person did wrong. But there is a time when the grieving has to come to an end, as does the punishment for the crime.

Four Reasons Not to Read This Book

Now let me point out four reasons why you should not read this book. If you are a father or a daughter who has these four expectations, my book will probably be a big disappointment.

#1   *You want my book to give you sure-fire ways to make other people change.*

There is an old joke among therapists: How many therapists does it take to change one light bulb? Only one, *but the light bulb has to want to be changed.* News flash: You are not a light bulb and neither is the person you are hoping to change. You cannot change other people. No book gives you recipes to make that happen. What you can change is your own behavior, your own beliefs, or your own expectations—and even that is no easy task. So if you are hoping that this book is going to give you some magic wand to change other people, you are going to be disappointed. This book is about you. But, like the light bulb, you have to *want* to be changed.

Yes, I will help you figure out what each of you would need to change to make things better between you two. I will tell you some things you do not want to hear. Sometimes I am going to rock the boat, because boat-rocking will help you pick up the oars and row your relationship to a better place. But you two are the ones who have to do the rowing.

#2   *You are hoping this book will confirm that you are not to blame for the difficulties in your father-daughter relationship. The blame and the shame lie with the other person, not with you.*

This book is not about blaming and shaming anyone. It may be true that one of you is guilty of having created a particular mess between you two. But even without knowing you, I am certain that both of you have said and done things over the years that strained or damaged your bond. So what? How does blaming or shaming the other person get you what you want, which is more joy and less stress between you two? In this book, I am going to be pointing out some of the mistakes each of you have made, as well as mistakes that mothers and stepmothers have made. My goal is to reduce the chances you will repeat those mistakes, not to give you ammunition to blame and shame each other.

#3 You do not want to read a book that makes you feel bad about yourself in any way.

If that is how you feel, this is not the book for you. This is not a "you go, girl" book where we women will "lean in" together against the men. Nor is it a "you're a great dad" book. I will be asking you both to step outside your comfort zone. Some of what I will be asking you to do might make you feel uneasy and maybe even a little guilty. But if you can tolerate feeling a little guilty or uneasy or sad, change is possible.

#4 You don't feel ready yet to work on your father-daughter issues—maybe later, but not now.

If so, you may want to come to grips with these realities. Most American men die before the age of 75, seven years sooner than women. By the time most daughters reach 50, their father is already dead. Time is running out. And it runs out faster for dads than for moms. If you keep dilly-dallying or making excuses, you may sadly discover that the very thing you need to strengthen your bond is the one thing you can no longer have: time together.

Why Bother? Is It Too Late?

If the troubles between father and daughter have been going on for some time, you might be wondering: is it too late to make things better? Is it worth the effort? Although there is never a guarantee that things will get better, consider this: if you do nothing differently, nothing will change. Reading what these real-life fathers and daughters have said after following my advice may give you the courage to try.

From the Dads

"I'm just a random person who was searching on the internet for a way to make things better with my daughter. I didn't think anyone understood what I was going through. This advice has been the tool kit I needed."

"I had no idea how to reconnect with my daughter since we hadn't spoken for so long. But Nielsen's advice opened the door. My daughter and I are talking again."

"I couldn't get my daughter to see me as anything other than this critical, uptight tyrant. But I've learned how to give her advice without upsetting her."

"My daughter would never share anything personal with me. I felt like an outsider in her life. Using Nielsen's suggestions, we're actually talking now about something other than politics and movies."

"As a dad I have finally found a book that includes my feelings and experiences. Nielsen has courageously gone where others fear to tread!"

"After I read this book, I sent a copy to my daughter. She's married with kids. So I figured she'd get angry at me, since that's what happens whenever I try to give her advice. To my surprise, she called to thank me."

From the Daughters

"Dr. Nielsen helped me jump-start the process of fixing my relationship with my dad after he got remarried to a woman I still don't like."

"I have finally gotten to know my father as more than an extension of my mother."

"I used to only think about my father in terms of me and how he affected my life. Now I think about how I affect his life."

"I feel pretty guilty and ashamed realizing I have been so hasty in judging my dad."

"When he told me he wished we talked more, I felt incredible. For the longest time I have wondered if he wanted more than our surface level conversations like I did."

"My father is a big man with a commanding presence that most people find intimidating, including me. But now that we're doing the quizzes and interviews in this book, I see him in a completely different way."

"Up until now, Dad and I had a fun but superficial relationship. I always went through mom to resolve my problems with him. That's not how it is anymore. It's more real and meaningful between us."

"Now I see my father as someone other than just a bald guy with his head in a book. Even as old as I am, I have a lot to learn from him. Who knew?"

"I've learned how to be alone with my father and ask personal questions. It was very moving when he said the best gift I've ever given him is wanting to get to know him."

"We finally talked about the things that have caused tension between us for years. As a mom now, I'm able to forgive the fact that he pretty much had to stumble through fatherhood."

"I didn't think my dad and I had much to improve on. I was so wrong. I have started getting to know him as a person, and we're actually talking like two grown-ups."

In bringing this chapter to a close, I am reminded of a cartoon. A distraught prisoner is shaking the bars of the prison cell door, desperately trying to escape. But to the left and to the right of the cell door, there are no bars. It is wide-open space. Freedom is literally just around the corner, if only the prisoner would stop rattling the bars and look to the right and the left. The message here is clear: we often imprison ourselves in a cell of our own making. We could set ourselves free, if only we would stop rattling the bars, calm down, take a step back, look around, and see the way out. Hopefully, my book will help you, as fathers and daughters, to see the way around some of the obstacles that are preventing you from creating a more comfortable, more open, more joyful relationship.

Chapter 1

The Four Steps for Father-Daughter Problem-Solving

"A backbone is more valuable than a wishbone."

Anonymous

Throughout this book, we will apply a four-step approach to resolving a wide range of father-daughter problems. These issues affect women and their fathers from the time daughters leave high school until their fathers' deaths. This chapter describes each step of this four-step approach. It also begins to lay out some of the practical techniques that can help women and their fathers overcome the stumbling blocks that are stressing or crippling their relationship. These four steps are intended for both fathers and for daughters, and use of the term "you" generally refers to both groups, not just to daughters or fathers.

★ Step 1: Consider the Research

The first step is to consider whether there are current research and national statistics that might help you understand more about the particular type of problem you are trying to solve. This information can be surprisingly useful. It may help put your troubling situation into perspective and may put some of your concerns to rest. Let's explore three situations that commonly create stress and distance between fathers and daughters where research data and current statistics may help you both.

As the daughter begins planning her wedding, tensions between father and daughter start to emerge over the costs. Who is going to pay for what? What is the price limit? How much debt is dad willing or able to take on if he pays for the kind of wedding she wants? In this situation, it is helpful to start with the facts about the average cost of weddings, how most couples handle the wedding expenses, and the financial concerns of fathers about incurring large debts for such "voluntary" expenses as weddings. Dad might discover that what his daughter is expecting him to contribute is very reasonable compared to what most weddings cost and lower than what most dads end up paying. On the other hand, the daughter might discover that most couples contribute far more to their wedding costs than she and her fiancée were planning to spend.

Or deep rifts might develop between father and daughter over lifestyle issues. Assume, for example, the daughter is planning to have a child with her live-in boyfriend. Dad is really rattled by this news. He not only believes this is "abnormal" in our society, but that these children will end up without a dad around. In this situation, having the most recent research is going to be useful. The dad would learn that having children without being married is not "abnormal" in our country. In the past decade, 40% of American children were born to unmarried parents.[1] On the other hand, the daughter is going to learn that unmarried parents are far more likely than married parents to separate. So yes, her dad is right that these children are a lot more likely to grow up without a dad in the home—or in their lives.[2] Being aware of this research, both father and daughter will have an easier time resolving the issue that is driving a wedge between them.

Now let's consider a third situation where research could be beneficial. A lesbian daughter tells her dad she plans to marry and have children with her partner. Dad can tolerate same-sex relationships, but not when it comes to raising children together. The father-daughter relationship is rapidly deteriorating, as dad blurts out: "It's just not fair to the kids. They won't be normal. And it's unlikely that your marriage is even going to last."

The research might help this dad and daughter a lot. He will learn that children raised by same-sex couples are just as well-adjusted as children raised by heterosexual parents, and that 60% of same-sex couples who live together are married.[2] And the daughter will learn that same-sex marriages are more likely to end in divorce than heterosexual marriages.[3] So Dad has a legitimate concern that his grandchildren will end up living apart from one of their parents.[3]

As these three examples illustrate, the first step in solving a father-daughter problem is to look for research about the concerns you each have. You don't have to be a research scholar to do this. You can use the internet to find websites of organizations that collect research and national statistics on your topic. You will find answers to some very specific questions in books written by scholars for the general public.

In the following chapters, I have taken this first step for you by providing research and statistics on a host of issues related to some of the most common difficulties between fathers and daughters. You will discover this research through "What Do You Think?" quizzes that help you compare your beliefs with what the data actually tell us. Discussing this research together can be the first step toward sorting things out between you.

★ Step 2: Don't Make Assumptions— Who Is This Man?

The second step is even more important than the first. Many daughters make assumptions about what their fathers feel or believe without first doing a reality check. A daughter jumping to conclusions about her father's beliefs and feelings can be self-defeating because, in many cases, her assumptions are wrong. Fathers can make incorrect assumptions too. But a father is far more likely to understand what his daughter's beliefs are and where they come from, because he has known her since she was born. In contrast, many daughters know very little about their fathers' lives, especially their childhoods. So in this book, the "Who Is This Man?" quizzes are designed to help daughters explore their fathers' beliefs and to understand the origins of those beliefs.

In the following three scenarios, each daughter jumps to conclusions without first finding out how her dad currently feels and what he currently believes about issues that are related to their particular difficulty. Each of these daughters assumes her dad is going to react badly if she tells him the truth about what she is doing or how she is feeling.

The first daughter is afraid to tell her dad that she is living with her boyfriend. She has been able to deceive her dad because she and her boyfriend still have separate apartments. But this is getting expensive, so they're planning to move in together. If she tells her dad the truth, will he stop helping her pay off her credit card debts?

The second daughter is bouncing off the wall because her divorced dad is getting remarried. She despises the woman. On top of that, her dad is no spring chicken, and he has health issues. So what about inheritance? Has Dad many any plans for insuring that the children from his first marriage inherit some of his wealth? Or will he allow the "wicked" stepmom to walk off with the lion's share?

The third daughter is in love with a man of a different race and religion. She's been able to keep this a secret from her dad because they live so far away from each other. Last year she and her dad had a big blowup over financial issues. If she tells him the truth about her boyfriend, will they be back in battle again?

These three daughters have jumped to the conclusion that there is going to be trouble if they are honest with their dads. They have already made their minds up that dad is going to react badly. They may be right. But they may also be wrong. How well do they really know their fathers? When is the last time each daughter talked to her dad about his views on any of the issues related to their current dilemma? Is the prediction of each daughter based on something her dad said or did years ago when she was much younger? Is she making assumptions based on what her mother or other people have said about her dad?

The crucial question is: how well does she *really* know her father? Is she willing to find out who he is now? Unless she has done a recent reality check, she might be on the wrong track. Being on the wrong track makes problem-solving infinitely more difficult. This is why a daughter needs to invest time—lots of time—in finding out: *who is this man?* What does he feel and believe—and *why*? Where do his beliefs and feelings come from? His parents? His religion? His experiences as an adult? Something he read? Things he has heard about other people's experiences?

In this second step, the *why* is more important than the *what*. Finding out *what* your dad believes is relatively simple and straightforward. The more interesting and more helpful question is *why* he feels this way. When you are listening to his answers to these questions, spend the most time exploring why he might have answered this way. The next vignette demonstrates this step in the four-step plan.

Lily is a lesbian daughter whose dad, Steve, is upset about her wanting to have children with her partner. Steve believes that same-sex couples should not raise children together. Lily jumps to the conclusion that her dad is a homophobic, prejudiced person. Maybe he is one of the people who voted against the marriage-equality proposition in their state several years ago. Come to think of it, she never actually asked him how he voted. One bad thought leads to the next. Maybe he is one of those people who is only pretending to be open-minded. Her unflattering assumptions are slowly driving a wedge between her and her dad. Here is where the *why* comes in. Why does he object to same-sex couples raising children together?

To her surprise, when she sits down and has a long conversation with her dad, Lily learns that his only concern is about the well-being of children. He voted for marriage equality. He favors laws that protect those in the LGBTQ community from any form of discrimination. He is not uncomfortable around gay or lesbian people. His only concern is for the children who are raised by gay or lesbian parents. Although Lily now understands the *why*, this does not mean her father is right. In fact, he is not right, as he will learn after completing Step One by looking at the research. The point is that this no longer has to drive a wedge between Lily and her dad. She can view him as a well-meaning person who needs educating, not as a hard-hearted homophobe.

To help fathers and daughters get the most out of this second step, I have created lists of questions in each chapter to guide daughters in "interviewing" their dads about their opinions and feelings on a wide range of topics—topics that you may seldom, if ever, have bothered to discuss with your dad. Your goal is to stop making assumptions about your father. These questions will show you *why* your dad feels and thinks the way he does about those issues that create tension between you two, and you will be in a better position to settle your disputes.

To benefit most from these conversations, there are several crucial things you need to put in place.

First, set aside plenty of private time together—*just the two of you*. Nobody, and I mean nobody, can be around, especially not any family member who can eavesdrop or keep popping in to interrupt you.

Second, choose a setting where nobody can interrupt you and where you are not easily distracted. No restaurants or cafés. You arrange to talk in your home, or you might take a long walk or go to a park. Choose a place where neither of you would be embarrassed if you were to get emotional.

Third, if you live too far apart to have this conversation in person, then Skype or talk by phone. Absolutely no texts or emails. That would defeat the purpose. You need to see and hear one another. From body language and tone of voice, you can get a better read on when to move forward and when to back off.

Fourth, daughters, if your dad seems to be struggling with a question or if he starts to clam up, you can encourage him with comments like: "Tell me more about that," or "Then what happened?" If he is really tensing up with a particular question, tell him that you can skip it or come back to it later if he wants. Remember, your goal is to open him up, not to shut him down.

Finally, the daughter should talk as little as possible. The goal is *not* to get to know one another better. The goal is for you to get to know your father better. If your dad says he wants to know how you feel about some of the questions, tell him you will be glad to talk with him later about that. But not now. The objective is to give your dad the entire stage, with you functioning as the friendly, encouraging, attentive interviewer.

★   Step 3: Identify and Share Your Fears

The third step is for each of you to identify and share your fears. Share your fears? Yes, share your fears. What do you fear might happen if you discuss "it"—that one topic that is creating tension or widening the gap between you? Specifically, what are you afraid you might lose if you discuss "it"? Why are you afraid to bring "it" up? Be very specific. This is not easy.

For example, these statements are too vague and not specific enough: "My fear is that we won't get along as well as we do now." "My fear is that things will get worse." In contrast, here are some specific fears. A daughter may fear her dad will cut her off financially. Either may fear the other will refuse to attend an upcoming family event or refuse to spend time together. Dad may fear his daughter will restrict his contact with grandchildren. Either of you may fear the other will badmouth and ridicule you to other people in the family. You need to put some time into figuring out what you specifically fear might happen if you bring "it" up for discussion. Following is an example of a father and daughter identifying their specific fears.

The "it" between Monica and her dad Sebastian is complicated. She wants to drop out of college, transfer to a technical school, and pursue a very different career path than the one her dad imagined for her. Her fear is that her dad will lose respect for her, become even closer to her older "successful" sister, and make her feel guilty for years to come by making comments that embarrass her in front of other people.

Fathers also have fears, of course. Sebastian fears that Monica is not going to earn enough money to support herself in the kind of lifestyle she has grown accustomed to unless she graduates from a four-year college. It's highly unlikely that the kinds of jobs she can get with a two-year degree will ever match the income of a college graduate. He also worries that there could be trouble ahead between the two sisters, who have always been a little jealous of each other. Since her older sister will be outdoing Monica in terms of income and lifestyle, what kind of strain will that put on their relationship?

Like Monica and her dad, you two have to figure out for yourselves why you are afraid to discuss the "it" that has come between you. Your challenge is to identify your fears in detailed, specific ways. For example, you might say, "I'm afraid if we talk about 'it,' it will drive us further apart." What exactly do you mean by "drive us further apart?" Try to imagine the worst that might happen in vivid detail. For example, the dad might refuse to attend his daughter's wedding, refuse to pay anything toward her college education, or leave her nothing in his will. Or the daughter might stop talking to her dad altogether, not invite him to her wedding, or refuse to let him see his grandchildren.

Once you figure that out, you need to share your fears with each other, being as specific as possible. Gulp, yes. The third step is that, when you get in touch with what it is that you fear, you have to put it right out there. Each of you has to put your cards face-up on the table.

What is the benefit of sharing your fears with each other? How is that going to help you find a solution to anything? First, it puts you on a more equal footing by showing that you are both vulnerable to being hurt. Sharing fears is disarming. Second, by stating your fears, you are giving the other person a chance to reassure you that your fear is unfounded. This is the chance for each of you to reassure one another that the fear is imaginary, not real: "No, I will definitely not do that to you. You don't need to be afraid of that happening." Third, even if either person admits that there is a possibility—or even a certainty—that what you fear would come true, you are still working toward solving the problem because you are still talking about it together. And even if you do not get a reassuring response that puts your fears to rest, at least you have a clearer idea how likely it is that your fear will come true.

Use the "My Fears Quiz" to help you figure out the "it" you are afraid to discuss. Imagine the three worst possible outcomes and three best possible outcomes. Then predict how likely you think it is that each of your worst and best outcomes might actually happen.

My Fears Quiz

1   What are three things you would like to discuss that might improve your relationship?
2   What are three of the worst things you could imagine might happen if you discussed "it?"
3   What are three of the best things you could imagine might happen if you discussed "it?"
4   How likely is it that each of these best and worst things would actually happen if you got up the courage to discuss "it?"
    1 = unlikely, 2 = 50/50 chance, 3 = almost certain

★   Step 4: Propose a Plan

In the fourth and final step, you will propose specific changes that each of you can make to reduce the strain that a particular situation is creating between you. There are three components to asking for change.

First, *only ask for one change.* Do not reel off a list of all the things you want the other person to change. Just focus on one, or maybe two, changes that you think would help resolve the situation.

Second, *tell one another how you feel about the troublesome situation as it now stands.* Sharing your feelings helps the other person understand *why* it is important to settle things between you. For instance, if the current situation makes you feel unloved, say so. Or if it makes you feel unappreciated or taken for granted, then say it. Sharing feelings also helps you perceive each other as vulnerable, sensitive people. Again, you want to be specific when you talk about your feelings. "I feel bad" or "I feel sad" is not very specific. Try these kinds of words instead to describe your feelings: unloved, unlovable, unappreciated, unwanted, abandoned, and rejected. Whatever your feeling is, own up to it and state it.

The third step is the hardest. *What are you going to do differently to contribute to a solution?* You need to make at least one change in exchange for the change that you are asking the other person to make. Both people have to contribute to the solution. It can't be all give on one side and all take on the other.

In the remainder of this book we will explore a host of father-daughter predicaments, using the four-step method to reach a solution. So remember:

#1   Consider the research.
#2   Don't make assumptions.
#3   Identify and state your fears.
#4   Propose a plan that includes one change you are willing to make.

Two Roadblocks to Success

The four-step approach will be much more successful if fathers and daughters recognize two common roadblocks that often get in the way. The first is asking for approval instead of asking for acceptance. The second is having negative, false beliefs about men as husbands, fathers, and communicators.

1) Approval vs. Acceptance

One of the most common stumbling blocks for fathers and for daughters is wanting and expecting *approval* instead of aiming for *acceptance*. When we seek approval, we are asking the other person to agree with our decisions or our beliefs. In essence, we are asking them to vote "yes" by affirming or applauding our decisions. Wrongly, many of us also equate approval with love: "If you really loved me, you would approve of my decisions. You would agree with my beliefs. You would affirm that what I am doing or what I am going to do is right and good."

Asking for and expecting approval is self-defeating and wrong-headed on several counts. First, asking for approval is often an unattainable, unreasonable request. The reality is that people do not always share the same beliefs, values, or goals, regardless of how much they love one another. Second, it is highly unlikely that we can change other people's deeply held beliefs or change their minds about big decisions. So in seeking someone's approval, you are often assuming you have the power to change the other person if you just try hard enough. Third, loving someone does not mean agreeing with his or her opinions or choices. Asking or expecting someone to prove they love or respect you by applauding your decisions or agreeing with your beliefs is childish and downright silly.

What we should be asking and striving for is *acceptance*. Acceptance means that we can freely and honestly voice our disapproval of one another's beliefs and decisions. But after we have aired our differences, we do not punish each other. By punish, I mean such things as harassing, mocking, ridiculing, shaming, withdrawing emotionally, or withholding money. Acceptance means we do not try to force other people to agree with us by making them feel unlovable or unloved. Above all, we do not blackmail each other emotionally by sending the message: "If you really cared about me, you would give me your approval." Acceptance, on the other hand means: We agree to disagree. Then we put it aside for the sake of our relationship.

Many fathers and daughters say they cannot accept the other's choices or beliefs because they think it means they are giving up their principles, or turning their backs on what they believe in. No, that is not what acceptance means. You do not have to abandon the principles you live by in your life in order to accept other people's rights to live by their principles. Acceptance does not mean putting your beliefs aside. It means not expecting or demanding that the other person abandon their decisions or their views because they do not reflect yours. In any relationship, there are times when we have to be accepting without ever being able approve. If we aimed for acceptance instead of approval, we would put less strain on our relationships.

Acceptance also means that we can wish the best for each other, even when there is no approval. Best wishes can be stated in any number of ways. "Just because I don't approve of what you're doing, doesn't mean I love or respect you any less." "I hope what you're doing turns out for the best. I really do." "Even though we can't agree on this, what matters most to me is your happiness. I want that for you with all my heart." All of us love and value certain people, even though we do not always agree or approve of their beliefs or choices. Fathers and daughters should be no exception.

2) False Beliefs About Men

The second roadblock is holding negative, untrue beliefs about men. When we believe negative stereotypes about any group of people—women, racial minorities, religious groups, physically or mentally disabled people, gay men or lesbians—those beliefs have a negative impact on how we interact with people who belong to those groups. The untrue beliefs that underlie the stereotypes—especially when those beliefs are popular in our society—influence our behavior and our expectations. Worse still, members of the stereotyped group sometimes believe the negative but false beliefs about themselves. For example, decades ago, it was widely believed that males were, by nature, better at math and science than females. The impact? Most girls and women steered clear of science and math courses and, as a consequence, seldom entered those types of jobs. This, in turn, reinforced the stereotype that females were not suited for these types of endeavors. Like men, women themselves were convinced they were not "wired" or "naturally suited" to succeed in math or science.

Similarly, there are a number of negative, unfounded stereotypes and popular myths about men that can have a negative impact on the father-daughter bond. Men as well as women often believe these damaging myths. Based on these false beliefs, the daughter and her father have negative expectations about what he is capable of as a parent. This is why it is so important that we recognize these powerful, but untrue, beliefs about men. The "Are Men Blockheads?" quiz will help you identify the false beliefs that might be having a negative impact on your father–daughter relationship. Which of these statements do you believe?

What Do You Think?

Are Men Blockheads? Which of these do you believe are true? Compared to women, men are generally . . .

____ less empathic and less sympathetic
____ less willing to compromise
____ less compassionate
____ less cooperative
____ less responsive and less sensitive to other people
____ less committed to personal and family relationships
____ less concerned about relationship problems
____ more judgmental and critical
____ more verbally aggressive
____ more domineering and rude in conversations

____ Your score (10 possible)

What was your score? Hopefully zero. None of these negative statements about men are true, based on decades of research on these topics.[4,5] Yes, there are men who are less empathic, less cooperative, and more judgmental and verbally aggressive than women. Maybe some of those men are in your family. But there are also women who are less empathic, less cooperative, and more judgmental and verbally aggressive than men, as you might also see in your family. Still, these individual cases based on your personal experiences do not change the fact that a large body of research conducted over several decades shows that males and females are generally alike in all of these ways. Men and women do not come from "different planets" in terms of communication, empathy, sensitivity, cooperation, verbal aggression, or compassion. In fact, there are more differences among women and among men in these respects than there are between men and women.

The take home message for fathers and daughters is this: men are just as empathic, sympathetic, cooperative and just as concerned about relationships as women. Men are not more verbally aggressive, more critical, or more judgmental than women. Men are just as good at communicating as women are, although they may communicate in different ways. For example, because men are socialized from the time they are young boys to hide their emotions, they are less likely than women to let others see that they are hurt, sad, rejected, or depressed.[6] This in turn means daughters might wrongly believe their fathers are less sensitive or less caring than their mothers when, in fact, the father is merely hiding his emotions, as he has been taught to do throughout his life. So if you are searching for the "big" differences between fathers and daughters in these regards, you will discover a molehill, not a mountain.

The point is that when fathers or daughters hold negative, untrue beliefs about men, this can limit and complicate their relationship. For example, if a daughter believes men are less compassionate and less sympathetic than women, she is less likely to turn to her father for personal advice or for comfort. This then deprives the dad of opportunities to share his sensitive, sympathetic, compassionate side with his daughter. Sadly, then, her negative but untrue beliefs about men are confirmed: men are not as sensitive and nurturing as women; or, more specifically: "My father is less sensitive and less nurturing than my mother." Just as most women once avoided math and science because we generally believed that females were not suited for those pursuits, a negative stereotype about fathers is confirmed because the daughter has not given her dad a chance to disprove it.

In short, stop stereotyping men and start identifying your false beliefs. Own up to them. Then stop giving those false beliefs control over your behavior and your expectations in your father-daughter relationship.

Will It Be Worth It?

Will the four-step approach and the other suggestions in this chapter work for you? If you make these changes, will things improve? As we discussed at the outset of this book, there are no guarantees that any particular method will improve people's relationships. But there is this guarantee: if you keep doing what you've been doing and keep waiting for something magical to come along with no effort on your part, it is highly unlikely that anything will improve. The comments from these real-life fathers and daughters should give you the courage to move your relationship forward by using the four-step approach.

What Daughters Say

"Dad said the best compliment I ever gave him was taking time to find out more about his past by asking him the questions in the quizzes."

"After taking a hard look at myself, I realize I have to stop pouting and walking away every time dad and I disagree about something."

"When he asks how I am, I have quit saying 'fine' when I'm not. I have to be willing to discuss 'it' when there is a problem between us."

"I've always felt my father was judgmental and uncaring because he's so businesslike when we talk. But after spending time alone with him asking the questions, I see that it's just a style that he's learned."

"I've got to stop clamming up and giving dad annoyed looks when I'm pissed at him."

"Listening to him talk about his feelings is hard for me. Yes, I know how unfair that is and I'm working on it."

"I often act annoyed and feel like he's prying when he tries to discuss anything personal. I'm embarrassed to admit that I've been cutting him off like this."

"I've had to admit to myself that I'm not very open and don't tell him my feelings. To hear him say he wants us to talk more when we're having a problem is somewhat scary to me. But I know I have to try if I want a better relationship."

"Now I see he isn't just the intellectual type who keeps everything to himself. I could tell when he was desperately searching for just the right thing to say to answer my questions."

What Fathers Say

"I've learned from talking to her that I don't need to jump right in there trying to give her advice. It feels odd to do that. But it's working."

"I ended up telling her about a few of the ways I screwed up when I was her age. I was really nervous. I was shocked when she thanked me for sharing these things with her. What a relief to know that I don't have to be perfect in her eyes."

"I always felt she didn't want to spend any time just with me. When I got up the nerve to tell her how much that hurt my feelings, she cried because she was feeling the same way—that I didn't want to spend any time alone with her."

"I didn't realize I always talked to her in such a businesslike way. So I've started trying to use a less serious, more friendly tone of voice."

"When I was answering her questions, I realized that my parents never allowed us kids to show anger. I think that's why I bottle up my anger and use guilt on my daughter when I'm mad at her."

"I wish I had been more personal and talked more with her when she was growing up. But it's never too late and I want this for both of us."

"I love that we have always been able to joke and talk about stupid things. But I see now that we never worked well together on the problems between us."

"I was really nervous talking to her about this serious stuff. I mean, we have never really talked alone like this before."

Reference List

(1) Geiger A, Livingston G. Eight facts about love and marriage in America. *Pew Research Center* February 13, 2019:1–2.

(2) Livingston G. The changing profile of unmarried parents. *Pew Research Center* April 25, 2018:1–5.

(3) Farrell W, Gray J. *The boy crisis: Why our boys are struggling and what we can do about it.* Dallas, TX: Ben Bella Press; 2018.

(4) Russell S, Fish J. Mental health in lesbian, gay, bisexual and transgender youth. *Annual Review of Clinical Psychology* 2016;12:465–487.

(5) Balliet D, Li N, Macfarlan S, Van Vugt M. Sex differences in cooperation: A meta-analytic review of social dilemmas. *Psychological Bulletin* 2011;137:881–909.

(6) Carothers B, Reis H. Men and women are from earth: Examining the latent structure of gender. *Journal of Personality and Social Psychology* 2012;104:385–407.

Chapter 2

Money Minefields and Misunderstandings

> When a fellow says, "It ain't the money, it's the principle of the thing," it's the money!
>
> Kin Hubbard, humorist, 1868–1930

> Money can't buy happiness. But it can make you awfully comfortable while you're being miserable.
>
> Clare Booth Luce, ambassador, author, 1903–1987

In this chapter we will be applying the four steps to father-daughter troubles that are directly or indirectly related to money and work. Problems that are directly tied to money are easy to spot. For example, how much money does the daughter expect her dad to spend on her college education or on her wedding? Other issues are indirectly tied to money: does the daughter view her dad as a workaholic who cares more about his career than about her? Are the two of them at odds about her future career? As we will see, in direct and indirect ways, issues related to money can create a wedge between fathers and daughters who otherwise get along very well.

Before we begin, it is worth noting that financial and career issues can draw fathers and daughters closer together. Consider these three famous, wealthy daughters who credit their fathers for their success—Lady Gaga, Taylor Swift, and Serena Williams.

Famous Daughters and Their Fathers: Money and Careers

Serena Williams, tennis champion, age 38, net worth $37 million, winner of four Olympic gold medals and more Grand Slams than any female player

Serena's father, Richard, started her playing tennis at the age of five. He was also her coach throughout most of her early athletic career. Serena has often lovingly praised her dad for the enormous contributions he made to her success: "He's been the most important person in my career."[1]

Lady Gaga, singer-songwriter, age 34, net worth $300 million, winner of nine Grammy Awards and two Golden Globe Awards

Lady Gaga, born Stefani Germanotta, shares 50% of her income with her father, Joe Germanotta. Her dad supported her career aspirations when she dropped out of college in her first year. He also bankrolled her for a year when she started her musical career. She frequently compliments her dad in the media, describing him as "my hero."[2]

Taylor Swift, singer-songwriter, age 31, net worth $350 million, winner of 10 Grammy Awards and one Emmy Award

Taylor's father, Scott, moved the family from Pennsylvania to Nashville so she could pursue her teenage dreams as a country music singer and songwriter. He also bought a stake in the production company that kick-started her career. In media interviews, she often describes him as "the perfect, supportive dad."[3]

Banking on Dad: Men's Money, Women's Love

Before taking the first step toward fixing a particular problem, fathers and daughters need to acknowledge a few uncomfortable realities about gender roles and money in our society. Focus on this sad reality: many men believe that how much money they earn affects the way women feel about them. They fear that women will find them less desirable or that wives and daughters will lose respect for them or admire them less if they do not earn "enough" money. Earning as large a salary as possible often becomes the yardstick for measuring their worth as husbands and fathers.

Are men correct? Do women—including their wives and daughters—love or admire men in part for their money? There is certainly enough research evidence to suggest the answer is *yes*. For instance, daughters whose dads help them out financially after they have finished their college educations are more likely to take care of their fathers in old age than daughters who do not receive financial help from their dads after they have finished their educations.[4] Most women also marry men whose incomes are higher than theirs. Rarely does a woman "marry down." She generally chooses a man with at least as much education and with a higher income than hers.[5] From the woman's perspective, this makes good sense financially, since only 25% of wives earn more money than their husbands.[6] Americans still expect men to be the main providers.[7] So it is no surprise that many husbands who earn less than their wives feel bad about themselves.[8] In short, men are not off-base in believing that women appear to love and admire them in part for their money.

Now what does this have to do with difficulties between fathers and daughters? First, if either of you believe that the "best" dads have to earn as much money as possible, then dad is likely to spend a lot of time away from his family trying to maximize his income. This, in turn, can lead to more distance between him and his daughter, as we will see later in this chapter. Second, dad or daughter might expect the dad to show how much he loves her through money—an expensive wedding, an education at a private college instead of a far less expensive state school, helping her pay off credit card debts after she finishes her education. If her dad cannot measure up, then what happens between them? Third, even after she finishes her education, the daughter might continue banking on dad—literally. She might expect him to continue helping her financially, whether helping her pay off credit card debts or putting money aside for her inheritance. If she is banking on dad, then financial issues are likely to complicate or strain their relationship.

The point is this: your father-daughter relationship exists in a society where many of us have placed a high value on the father's income. This, in turn, can create obstacles between fathers and daughters. Keeping these realities in mind, let us now look at some of the money issues that fathers and daughters face.

The College Years: The Money Drain

Not surprisingly, issues surrounding the cost of the daughter's college education can create stress. These issues include how much dad and daughter will each contribute financially to her education and living expenses, how the money is to be spent, and how many years the dad will keep helping her financially once she becomes a young adult. College-age daughters want their fathers to treat them like adults. Yet many of them rely completely on their dads for money. Daughters need to ask themselves: "How can I expect dad to treat me like a grown-up unless I am willing to shoulder at least some of the financial burden for my education? If dad is going to continue supporting me for these next few years, then how much of a say should he have in how I spend that money?" And dads need to ask themselves: "How much is too much—not just how much money am I going to keep giving my daughter, but for how many years?" There is no right answer to these questions. And that's exactly the point: fathers and daughters need to discuss these issues and reach a mutual agreement *before* the college years begin.

Let's start with Rachel and her dad, Dave, who are arguing about her college expenses and about her future career plans—arguments they have had since she started college. As usual, they end up arguing about her grades, sorority bills, and her unpaid summer internships.

Dave feels like a banking machine. He sees her as being irresponsible, spending too much money, and not working hard enough to make good grades at the expensive college that she insisted on attending. Dave thought she would do her best and be a serious student. Instead, she spent a lot of time with her sorority activities. Her grades suffered. When he asks her about her grades or future career plans, she explodes. Meanwhile, Dave has had to take out pretty big loans to cover her college expenses.

As Dave puts it, "Why am I spending all this money on college when she's goofing off? Can't she see what I'm sacrificing for her? On top of that, she chose some goofy major that isn't going to lead to a decent-paying job." Dave can also see more trouble ahead. Rachel and her mom are already starting to talk about the big graduation festivities next year. Her mom has already told her that they will pay for her summer abroad program. Rachel and her mom have also been talking about Rachel living at home the year after she graduates without having to spend any of her income for living expenses. Dave feels that this is babying Rachel and undermining her autonomy.

Rachel fluctuates between feeling grateful and feeling angry, guilty, and embarrassed. "I think Dad looks at me and sees nothing but a big dollar sign. He lashes out at me for stupid little things like my sorority bills. I've thanked him for his support. What more does he want? He's always putting me on a guilt trip. I've even heard him complaining to mom about me, which really made me feel awful." To make matters worse, Rachel's older sister graduated from college with honors and landed a great job after earning a master's degree.

Rachel wants her dad to see her as competent and responsible and to stop treating her like a little girl. But all last summer, Dave made snippy little comments about how she never made any money. He's always asking about her grades and future career plans. She feels it's not her fault that the work she does during the summers is volunteer work with no pay. She sees it as resume-building. She knows she played around too much in her first year in college. But she doesn't think her grades or career plans are any of her dad's business. She knows she's not measuring up to her dad's expectations. So even though she's irritated with him, she can't stand the thought of his being disappointed or ashamed of her.

★ Step 1: Consider the Research

The first step is to consider the research that might be relevant to what you're dealing with. As the old saying goes: "Get the facts first. You can distort them later." Rachel needs to see how she scores on the following research quiz.

What was your score? The perfect score is zero. All of these statements are false, according to our most recent research and national surveys. Are you surprised? The next section presents the research in a nutshell.

The Research: Myths About Men

- When kids are under the age of five, moms do roughly two-thirds of the direct childcare because dads do two-thirds of the financial childcare.[6]
- In 2015, couples with a family income of $60,000–$100,000, spent $217,000 raising one child to age 18 and those earning over $100,000 spent up to $400,000 per child.[9]
- Most men do not have a choice to work fewer hours because of the family's financial needs and competition at work.[10]
- Most dads wish they could spend less time at work and more time with their kids.[10–12]
- Less-educated dads feel worse than college-educated dads about spending too little time with their children.[11]
- When both parents work fulltime, dads spend about 30 minutes less a day with their kids than moms do.[12]

What Do You Think?

Quiz 1: Men, Work, and Money

Which of these do you think are true?

___1   The average cost of raising one child to age 18 is $160,000 for middle-income parents.

___2   Most dads are satisfied with the amount of time they spend at work and with their kids.

___3   When both parents work full-time, dads spend about half as much time with kids as moms.

___4   Most men place a higher priority than women do on work than on family.

___5   Dads are less stressed than moms trying to balance work and family.

___6   Moms are putting in more hours than dads to meet the family's needs.

___7   Dads are not as happy or as relaxed as moms when they're spending time with the kids.

___8   The main reason moms do most of the childcare is that most dads refuse to do it.

___9   In most families the mother does almost all of the grocery shopping.

___10   Men who hold traditional gender roles spend the least time with their kids.

___11   Most wives feel their husbands are mistreating them in terms of sharing the childcare.

___12   Most Americans believe moms should contribute as much as dads to the family's income.

___13   When children are under the age of five, most moms have full-time jobs.

___14   Very few women with a college degree are stay-at-home moms.

___15   College-educated dads feel worse than less-educated dads about not spending enough time with their kids.

_____ Your Score

- Forty percent of Americans still believe the dad should earn most of the family's money.[12]
- About 28% of men and 25% of women put a higher priority on work than on family.[13]
- Only 22% of married couples say dad is more career-oriented than mom.[14]
- Dads have as much or more stress as moms trying to balance work and family.[12,14]
- Counting paid and unpaid work, parents spend equal time meeting the family's needs.[15,16]
- Dads are happier and more relaxed than moms when spending time with the kids.[17]
- The more equal their hours at work, the more equal the childcare and housework.[14,18]
- Most parents share the grocery shopping. [19,20]
- There is no strong link between gender-role beliefs and fathering time. [21,10]
- Most mothers feel the division of paid and unpaid work in their family is fair.[22]
- Only 16% of adults believe moms should work fulltime, and only 42% believe moms should work part-time when the kids are young.[23]
- Only 35% of moms work fulltime when children are under the age of five.[24]
- Thirty percent of stay-at-home moms have a college degree.[25]

Why should Rachel or any of us care what the research says? Because when fathers or daughters hold false beliefs, their biases and stereotypes make it more difficult to build strong bonds and to settle their differences. As explained in Chapter One, when we have negative beliefs about any group of people—whether it is fathers, men, or racial and religious minorities—we're wearing blinders that complicate our relationships with each other.

★ Step 2: Don't Make Assumptions

Rachel's next step is to find out more about her dad's feelings and life experiences. Before making negative assumptions about him, and instead of just relying on what her mother has told her about him, Rachel needs to try to put some pieces of the puzzle together for herself. So she goes on a fact-finding mission about his beliefs in terms of work, money, and dreams by asking him the questions in the following "Who Is This Man?" quiz.

Rachel might start with something along these lines: "Dad, I've been thinking lately about how little we've ever talked about your opinions and feelings about money and work. I'd really like to know more about you. I've even made a list of questions that really interest me about your life. How about I send them to you, and you tell me when you'd like to talk about them?"

Who Is This Man?

Quiz 1: Work, Money, and Dreams

1   When you were growing up, what influenced your attitudes about money?
2   How much did your parents help you financially after you graduated from high school?
3   How well do you think you lived up to your dad's expectations?
4   Did you ever feel your parents didn't treat you fairly when it came to money?
5   When you were my age, what were your hopes in terms of work and money?
6   When you were younger, what mistakes do you think you made about work or money?
7   What do you wish you had known about work and money earlier in your life?
8   How and why have your views about money and work changed over the years?
9   Have you ever felt someone loved or respected you partly because of your income?
10   What are your hopes and your worries about me in terms of work or money?
11   What would you like me to learn from you about money and work?
12   How responsible do you feel for the decisions I make about work and money?
13   If I'm not successful financially or don't land a good job, do you feel it's your fault?
14   How do you feel about each of your children's accomplishments so far in life?
15   What worries you about my generation when it comes to work or money?

Dave finds it easy to answer the questions that are not particularly personal. He easily tells stories about the people and events that influenced him, how he paid for college himself, and how his ideas about work and money have changed over the years. He chatters on about lessons he hopes she will learn about money and about things he wishes he'd known earlier in his life about work. But he gets uncomfortable and a little annoyed with questions that are related in any way to his father or to Rachel and her sister. He turns from a chatterbox into a locked box.

As explained in Chapter One, Rachel can handle her dad's discomfort in several ways. The first move is to acknowledge what is happening. "Dad, you're clamming up when I ask you anything about your father. Is there some reason you don't want to talk about him with me?" Based on his answers, she needs to find a way to put him at ease. For example, Dave might say that talking honestly about his dad is hard because he doesn't want Rachel to think less of her grandfather. Then Rachel might say, "Dad, I'm old enough to know that nobody is perfect. If getting to know you means hearing some negative things about Grandpa, I can handle that." If she cannot get him to relax and talk freely, she can simply offer him the option of skipping the question. "Since it's making you so uneasy, do you want to just skip this question?"

Most of us have developed our own unique ways of helping other people open up and talk about difficult topics. Some of us are good at joking and getting the person to laugh. Or we might share something personal about ourselves to get the ball rolling. Whatever Rachel's particular strategies are, she'll use them when she sees her dad getting tense or uneasy.

★ Step 3: Identify and Share Your Fears

Dave feels unloved in the sense that he feels his daughter uses him as a banking machine. He feels unappreciated and taken advantage of financially. He does not feel Rachel is being very compassionate or sympathetic. He is also afraid for Rachel because it does not look as if she's going to be able to take care of herself financially in the future. In a way, he feels he has failed as a parent to prepare her for the future.

Rachel feels unloved in the sense that she believes her dad thinks less of her because of her poor grades. She feels like an embarrassment to him. She fears she is going to look even worse in his eyes if she doesn't get her act together about her future. She has always felt she had to compete with her sister for their dad's respect and attention. And now there's no doubt that she is losing the competition.

★ Step 4: Propose a Plan

The following is a sample of an ideal conversation between Dave and Rachel. By ideal I mean that in each conversation both of them are honest about how they feel and what they fear. Then they each specify exactly what behaviors they would like changed. Being specific is crucial. For example, "be nicer to me" or "stop hassling me" are not specific. But "thank me more often" or "don't say anything more about how much money you've spent on me" are specific.

Ideally, Dave reassures Rachel that he loves her no matter what grades she makes or what job she ends up with after she graduates. He admits that he is hurt because he feels like her banking machine. He also admits that he feels he hasn't done a good job preparing her. He tells her that he's afraid she'll pull further away from him if he doesn't keep doling out money, or if he refuses to let her live at home for free after she graduates. Without criticizing the mother, he lets her know how hurt he is when she goes to her mom instead of talking things over with him.

Once his fears and feelings are out in the open, he offers up a plan, asking for three very specific changes. First, he promises not to complain any more about her college expenses if she agrees to get a paying job for the next two summers. Second, he promises not to ask any more about her grades or future career plans, as long as she will come to him from time to time and fill him in on what's going on. "Keep me in the loop instead of just going to your mom to talk about these things." Third, he asks that, when she gets closer to graduation, she sits down with him and her mom together to talk about whether she'll live at home for free after she graduates.

Rachel begins by reassuring her dad that she does appreciate all he has done for her and knows how much stress he is under financially. Then she explains that she feels angry and guilty when he keeps asking about her grades and future plans or keeps reminding her what she costs him. She tells him that she thinks he is ashamed of her and thinks she is a loser. She even gets up the courage to ask: "Dad, do you think I'm a loser compared to my sister? Are you ashamed of me?"

After sharing her feelings, she offers a plan: "If you'll stop asking me about my grades and future plans, I promise I'll come to you to talk things over." She also asks if he could boost her confidence by letting her know every now and then that he's not ashamed of her—reassuring her that she is just as loved and just as lovable as her sister.

Of course, no two fathers and daughters are the same. But if you follow the four steps, at the very least you will get your feelings and requests out into the open. And if your initial plan doesn't work out, you can always come back and fine-tune it. As the old saying goes, "you're never going to catch a fish if you won't even put your line in the water."

Daughters' Reactions

Each father and daughter have to create a plan that works for them and meets their particular needs. Some of them will not be able to reach an agreement. But if that happens, it doesn't mean that the daughter wasted her time talking to her dad about his life and getting to know him better. As you can see from these daughters' comments, discovering more about their fathers helped them put together more pieces of their father puzzle.

"I used to get mad when he would say anything about how much money he's had to spend for our college educations. Now I see that he's not being selfish. He'd just like to be able to retire at 65."

"I used to feel that whenever my dad looked at me, all he could see was a big dollar sign. But I see now that I've made him feel like a big wallet because almost every time I call him, I'm asking for money."

"I understand why he is so sharp with me. He resents having had to drop out of college. And even though it isn't fair, it spills over onto me."

"I'm going to stop assuming I know how he feels without asking him first. And if I want him to open up, I have to be willing to do it too."

"My father grew up in the Caribbean where a good father provides money without the need to be emotionally present. So in my family nobody says 'I love you.' But when he was answering my questions, I realized that despite his upbringing, he wants to be more emotionally involved in my life."

Daughters' Weddings

Fathers and daughters can also run into trouble when it comes to the cost of big events like graduations and weddings. In most families, the most expensive and most emotional event is the daughter's wedding. Savannah and her dad, Gregg, are both excited about her recent engagement. Gregg likes his future son-in-law. He is also glad that his daughter and her fiancé each have the kind of jobs that will allow them to have a better standard of living than he ever had—or will ever have. Savannah is the first of his two daughters to get married. Wedding planning is a new experience for the family.

Everything was going well until it got down to the nitty-gritty of making the actual plans for the wedding. When Savannah showed her dad the price tag for her dream wedding, Gregg went into sticker shock. If he gives his daughter what she wants, he will have to take out a sizeable loan. Thinking ahead, he also realizes that whatever he gives Savannah, he's going to have to give her sister when the time comes for her wedding. Although this thought hasn't crossed Savannah's mind, her dad is having to make two big financial decisions, not just one. And since her mom doesn't work, all of the financial burden for weddings falls on her dad. To complicate things even more, her mom has always been somewhat of a spendthrift. As expected, she hasn't voiced any concerns about the wedding costs. In fact, she and Savannah seem to be on a feeding frenzy—feeding each other more and more lavish ideas for the wedding. Based on his prior experience with Savannah and her mom, Gregg knows he's going to be portrayed like a cheapskate if he dares to complain—and, worse than that, if he flat out says "no" to giving Savannah as much money as she (and her mom) are expecting from him.

He fears that both his wife and his daughter are going to turn against him unless he caves in. He also fears his other daughter might side with "the women" and wield her favorite weapons against him: the cold shoulder, the snide remarks, and her favorite stab, "if you were a woman, you would understand." At the same time, he wonders why Savannah is being so insensitive. Why can't she have a less-expensive wedding like her cousin recently had? That was a perfectly lovely wedding, with plenty of special touches that didn't cost an arm and a leg. Besides, when he and her mom got married, their wedding didn't leave anyone in debt. Gregg also wonders: is a father's love being measured by how much he spends on his daughter's wedding? For that matter, are Savannah and her mom gullible victims of a wedding industry that implants the idea—especially in young girls—that the more expensive the wedding, the greater the love between bride and groom or bride and father of the bride? And why can't she and her fiancé take on more of the financial burden here? In fact, since her fiancé is an only child, why can't his parents chip in more? Why can't Savannah think far enough ahead to realize how long it's going to take her dad to pay off the wedding loan?

Meanwhile Savannah is hurt, confused, and angry. She knows her dad loves her. And they have always gotten along well, except for the battles during her teenage years. So why is he being so stingy and so uptight about the wedding costs?

The good news is that this conflict does not reflect any major problem in the father-daughter relationship itself. The conflict is clearly focused on how much money to spend for one specific event. The tension stems from the fact that Savannah and her dad have different values, different expectations and different long-range concerns when it comes to one specific situation: the cost of her wedding. But, because this is a highly emotional occasion that carries such great weight in our society, if they do not handle this well, it could create bad feelings between them that would last well past the wedding.

★ **Step 1: Consider the Research**

The first step is for Savannah and her dad to look at the research that might shed light on their situation. She needs to understand what her dream wedding would mean in terms of the big picture for her parents. And Gregg needs to understand what weddings today cost.

What Do You Think?

Quiz 2: Today's American Wedding

Which ones do you think are true?

___1	Most couples pay for their weddings themselves.
___2	Most weddings cost about $33,000.
___3	The biggest expense is renting the space.
___4	Most couples hire a professional wedding planner.
___5	Most wedding celebrations last 2–3 days.
___6	Almost half of all couples spend more than budgeted.
___7	The average wedding gown costs about $1,500.
___8	Most couples invite about 140 people.
___9	The average cost for the photographer is $2,500.
___10	The average rehearsal dinner costs about $1,300

_____ Your Score

Which ones did you think were true? The correct answer is: all of them. Compare your answers to the following facts from a 2017 national survey of nearly 14,000 brides.[26]

The Research: Surprise

- $33,093: Average price of a wedding in 2017
- Sixty-eight percent use professional florists and decorators.
- Eighty percent have a cocktail hour.
- Eighty percent of wedding celebrations last two to three days.
- Eighty-four percent have a rehearsal dinner.
- Thirty-five percent have a post-wedding brunch.
- Forty-nine percent have registries for gifts that include giving cash.
- Forty-five percent went over their planned budget.
- Nine percent paid for their entire wedding themselves.

The average costs were:

- $15,000: venue rental fee
- $2,600: photographer
- $2,000: wedding planner
- $2,000: videographer
- $528: cake
- $1,300: rehearsal dinner
- $5,680: engagement ring
- $1,631: wedding gown
- $260: cost per guest

★ Step 2: Don't Make Assumptions

To get a better grip on her dad's feelings and fears, Savannah needs to have some long, private conversations with him. She can start with the questions that Rachel asked her dad—basic questions about work and money. Then she can move on to the more specific questions about weddings. She and her dad should definitely be looking at her parents' wedding pictures when they have this conversation.

As Savannah expected, Gregg was slow to warm up to this question-answer conversation. After all, it is the first time the two of them have spent one-on-one, private time talking about a serious topic. It is also the first time Savannah has ever had a specific list of questions entirely focused on Gregg talking about his life and his feelings. In

Who Is This Man?

Quiz 2: Weddings

1 What was your wedding like?
2 How was your wedding paid for?
3 What was the saddest wedding you ever attended?
4 What do you wish could have been different about your wedding?
5 How did you and mom go about making decisions for your wedding?
6 How is the kind of wedding I want different from what you were hoping I'd want?
7 What are the most important parts of a wedding in your mind?
8 What were the best and the worst parts of your wedding?
9 What worries you the most about my wedding?
10 If you had the money, what would you want for my wedding?
11 Do you wonder if I'll think less of you if you can't pay more for my wedding?
13 How do you think your role is different from mom's role in my wedding?
14 Do you feel left out in any way in my wedding planning?

other families, the mother would probably be involved in this talk about wedding costs. But Savannah's mom has opted out and left the decision making to Gregg.

The easiest questions for Gregg are the ones about his own wedding. Having his wedding pictures in hand makes it even easier to tell the stories. The two of them end up laughing a lot at his wedding pictures, especially at everyone's hairstyles and clothes. But then Gregg tenses up as the questions shift to the fact that he doesn't earn enough money to give her the kind of wedding she wants. Savannah realizes that even though Gregg is acting annoyed with her about the wedding costs, he's mainly feeling embarrassed about his income. Somehow, she has to find a way to get to the heart of it. She might explore his feelings with a calm, comforting voice: "Dad, I'm getting the feeling that you wish you made a lot more money. Is that what's going on?" Or, "Are you afraid that I'm going to admire or love you less because you're not as rich as my fiancé's dad? Could you tell me what I could say or do to show you that isn't true?"

★ Step 3: Identify and Share Your Fears

Gregg fears that if he caves to Savannah, he and her mom will have financial struggles in the future that they might not easily be able to overcome. On the other hand, his bond with Savannah means the world to him. He's afraid that if he doesn't give her what she wants, it will weaken their bond. Savannah fears that she's going to lose her once-in-a-lifetime chance to have the wedding of her dreams. She also fears that she might resent her dad in certain ways if he isn't going to help make her dream come true. If she has to settle for less, even if she tries her best to put it aside, what if she finds herself feeling disappointed or sad after the wedding is over? And what if she holds her dad responsible?

★ Step 4: Propose a Plan

Because they have always been close and relaxed together, it is fairly easy for them to share their feelings and their fears. Neither Gregg or Savannah feel unloved or unappreciated. This father-daughter pickle has nothing to do with Savannah feeling jealous or competitive with her sister, which was a complicating factor for Rachel and Dave. But, like Rachel and Dave, both Savannah and Gregg are afraid that this financial disagreement might somehow damage their connection.

After telling each other how they feel, Gregg and Savannah discuss a number of options. Gregg raises the idea of asking her future in-laws to contribute a greater amount of money. Savannah quickly rejects that idea. He also suggests that she ask people to give money as gifts instead of buying actual gifts. This is already offered as an option on most wedding registries. But that is something she and her fiancé have already done. Savannah suggests that she would be willing to pay for part of her sister's wedding when that time comes. Gregg rejects this because it might make her sister uncomfortable and because there is no way to guarantee that she would have the money. She also asks her dad to reconsider whether having to retire a year or two later would really be such a burden.

The bottom line is that Savannah and her dad both have to accept the reality that this dream wedding is only going to happen if people make some pretty big financial sacrifices. Savannah's parents' financial situation is what it is. They aren't suddenly going to become wealthy enough to cough up the money for this wedding. So the questions they need to discuss are: depending on who makes what sacrifices, how do we think it's likely to affect our relationship? For example, if Savannah and her fiancé pay more and get their dream wedding, will she resent her dad? Can she let go of her disappointment? Or if Gregg doesn't give her as much as she's asking for, will he feel guilty afterwards—if so, for how long? Nobody can predict how they will feel after the wedding is over and the bills come pouring in. And neither can know whether their feelings are going to be long-lasting or short-lived.

At the end of their talk, neither of them got exactly what they wanted. Gregg agreed to take out a loan, but not for the full amount Savannah was counting on. Savannah compromised by cutting back some of the honeymoon plans so that she and her fiancé could put more money into the wedding. She couldn't help but envy her recently married friend whose dad had paid for all of her expensive wedding. Wisely, though, Savannah kept her feelings to herself. She was able to hold back because she had taken the time to ask her dad the questions about his life. Otherwise, she would not have known how ashamed he had always felt for never achieving what he had hoped for as a young man. In his own eyes, he is a financial loser. What's the point of making him feel worse by putting him on a guilt trip?

Daughters' Reactions

There is no one-size-fits-all answer to wedding related headaches like these. But whatever the outcome, taking time to explore their father's feelings and his beliefs often has unexpected rewards for daughters:

> "At the beginning of our talk, he was sitting with his legs and arms tightly crossed. But by the end his feet were propped up, his arms were on the armrests, and he looked so comfortable."

> "It made me so sad to hear him say that even when he was my age, he had no dreams for the future. He even looked sad talking about his wedding pictures. I got a glimpse into the darkness and emptiness inside him."

> "I've started seeing my father as a person who struggles through life as a man, and a husband, not just as my father."

> "I only thought about my father in terms of how his actions affected me—not how I affected him. I never thought about him as a person with his own dreams and problems having nothing to do with me."

The Workaholic Dad, the Superficial Relationship

Unlike Savannah and Gregg, there are fathers and daughters who have a distant, detached relationship with each other. They do not argue much because they rarely talk about anything difficult or controversial. Many of these fathers are highly successful at work and earn such high incomes that their wives do not work at all or only work part-time. As a consequence, many of these daughters are much closer to their mothers than to their fathers—a situation we will discuss in detail in the next chapter. Work and money can have a profound impact, as we can see in Paul and Molly's situation.

Paul is a relatively wealthy, highly successful lawyer who has never held back spending money on his family. Molly's mom never worked outside the home and is closer to all of the children than Paul is. Paul has always been a workaholic who desperately wants to become a senior partner at his firm. Even at his age, he still works at least 60 hours a week. When Molly was 10, Paul rented an apartment in the city because commuting from the suburbs was too exhausting. He was only able to come home on weekends. Molly has always felt her dad cared too much about work, money, and status. She also thinks he brags too much about his accomplishments and is somewhat arrogant. Still, whether on the golf course, at work, or in the community, he is widely admired for his intelligence and for his financial generosity with charities and with friends.

Now that Molly is about to become a mother, she and her husband are worrying about the negative impact that Paul's money might have on their lives. They are thinking back to their wedding, where Paul insisted on a very lavish event which is not what Molly and her fiancé wanted. Things had gotten pretty tense, but they let Paul have his way. Molly felt her wedding became an expensive showcase for Paul. And she worries that this same sort of thing might happen once he becomes a grandfather. She and her husband worry that Paul will spoil their child with lavish gifts, expensive birthday parties, and extravagant vacations. They know that Paul believes in the "golden rule"—he who has the gold, makes the rules. And they also know that in the past they have not stood up to him when he goes overboard spending money on them. Molly admires her dad's success. But she sees him as too materialistic and superficial. He reminds her of the cartoon where the rich man's last words on his death bed are, "I wish I'd bought more crap."

As Molly explains, "When I'm talking, I can tell his mind is a million miles away. I can't imagine our talking about anything other than his work and the next expensive thing he plans to buy. Even now, when he asks me how I am, I just say 'fine' and change the subject. To be honest, he doesn't know much about my life. He never really did. I remember once in fourth grade a classmate asked me if my parents were divorced because I never talked about my dad and he never showed up at events. I was embarrassed because other people had noticed that my dad was never around." Molly also admits that, even at her age, she feels a little jealous of the bond that some of her friends have with their dads.

Paul comes from a working-class family where his parents fought a lot about money. He prides himself on the fact that his wife has never had to work the way his mom did. Paul sees himself as a great provider, which to him is the same as being a great husband and father. Sadly though, he thinks women's love depends in part on how much money men make. As he often says, only half-jokingly: "When a man's money stops coming in the door, a woman's love flies out the window."

As Paul puts it, "I've worked my ass off making money for my family. I'm glad I can give my wife and kids more than my dad was ever able to give us. As for Molly, she never wanted much to do with me. Even now, she is standoffish and can be a little snarky. I mean, a few years ago when we were making plans for her wedding, it seemed like the more money I spent on her, the snippier she got." When he talks about soon becoming a grandfather, he often brags about all the things he plans to do for his first grandchild—meaning things that money can buy, of course.

★ Step 1: Consider the Research

Molly's first step is to consider the relevant research. How many of the statements in the following quiz do you think are true?

What was your score? Which ones did you think were true? The first five are true. The next five are false. Here's what the research says.[10, 27–30]

The Research

- When husbands work more than 60 hours a week, their wives are three times more likely than other women to quit work.[27]
- Twenty percent of fathers but only 6% of mothers work at least 50 hours a week.[30]
- When both parents work fulltime, most dads spend seven more hours at work than moms.[31]
- The most stressful years at work are for people in their 30s and early 40s.
- Most college-educated men make their greatest career contributions well before the age of 50.[23]

- Highly successful, higher income men have a harder time adjusting to retirement than other men.[32]
- Most women still choose to enter family friendly jobs that require less time at work and have more flexible hours than men's jobs.[28]
- American men die seven years before women, partly because of job-related health problems and injuries at work.[33]
- When men and women work more than 50 hours a week, they earn equivalent incomes.[28]

What Do You Think?

Quiz 3: Fathers' and Mothers' Jobs

Which statements are true?

___1   Workaholic dads are the most likely to be married to stay at home wives.

___2   Men are more likely than women to have time-consuming, demanding jobs.

___3   Even when both parents have full-time jobs, dads generally work more hours that moms.

___4   America has the worst father-friendly workforce policies of any industrialized country.

___5   Men die sooner than women in part because of job related health problems.

___6   College educated dads generally reach their career peak in their late 50s.

___7   The more successful a dad is in his career, the more content he will be as it winds down.

___8   Dads with the highest incomes adapt better to retirement than less wealthy dads.

___9   The most stressful years at work for most fathers are in their early 50s.

___10   Most women choose jobs that are just as demanding and time consuming as men's jobs.

_____ Your Score

★ Step 2: Don't Make Assumptions

Now that she has considered the research, Molly needs to arrange a private time to ask her father questions that can help her understand his feelings and views. Molly needs to ask her dad the questions in the previous "Who Is This Man?" quiz as well as the questions that follow.

Because her dad is such a workaholic and is somewhat aloof and arrogant, Molly assumed their conversation would be like a business meeting—impersonal, stilted, and brief. And for the most part, she was right. Paul was a little smug and sometimes ended up lecturing her when he answered questions about his work and money. When he talked about how people have misunderstood him at work, he seemed to be blaming everyone but himself. Molly felt herself getting annoyed as he bragged and kept reminding her of all he had sacrificed for the family. She was also hurt when he said his three most important possessions were the house, the new car, and his extraordinarily expensive watch.

On the other hand, as the conversation went on, he made a few surprising confessions. He admitted that he always wanted to be a professor, not a lawyer. But the pay was too low. He also opened up about being embarrassed as a child because his dad "wasn't ambitious enough" and "didn't amount to much." It struck her as sad that Paul said he most wanted to be remembered after he died for being a wonderful husband and father. This was so at odds with his focus on work, money, and success. He didn't see the disconnect between how he lives his life and what it takes to build close, meaningful bonds with your family. Even though he said he wished he had spent more time with the family, he didn't sound very regretful. And nothing he said indicated that he planned to cut back on work even as he ages.

As they were talking, Molly realized she had been hoping her dad would surprise her by giving insightful, introspective answers to some of the questions. He didn't. He never fully relaxed, even after a second glass of scotch. For someone as at ease and as confident as he is at work, he was surprisingly tense and awkward answering the questions. Although his answers were not especially meaningful, Molly came away with several new insights. He sounded a little lost, confused, and fragile when trying to answer questions about his future. He seemed the most rattled and the most vulnerable when the questions had anything to do with aging or retirement. He even repeated something he heard a comedian say: "I don't want to achieve immortality through my work. I want to achieve it through not dying." Molly came

Who Is This Man?

Quiz 3: Work, Values, and Success

1. As you were growing up and as a young adult, who influenced the type of work you chose?
2. If money hadn't mattered at all, what kind of work would you have chosen and why?
3. What have you liked least and liked most about your work over the years?
4. Do you consider yourself too perfectionistic, too self-critical, or too focused on work?
5. How do your parents, your wife, and your siblings feel about the work you do?
6. What have people misunderstood about you in terms of your job or money?
7. What do you wish had been different about your job when I was growing up?
8. How do you define success and how successful do you think you are?
9. If you could afford to retire now, would you? Why?
10. What are your proudest accomplishments at work?
11. How do you define happiness and what role do work and money play in that?
12. What have you had to give up over the years because of your job?
13. What do you hope for in the remaining years of your career?
14. What are some of the most meaningful compliments you've gotten about your work?
15. How worried are you about the effects that aging might have on your work some day?
16. What are three of your most important possessions?
17. What would make you happiest in the next few years?
18. Who have you loved or admired who did not have a highly successful career or big income?
19. What do you hope people will remember most about you after you retire?
20. How do you feel about your financial role as a grandparent?

away with the sense that her father is in many ways like the child she will soon have—a person who sometimes feels vulnerable and afraid and confused, but hides it—a person who goes about trying to get people to love or respect him in all the wrong ways and doesn't have a clue why things aren't working out.

★ Step 3: Identify and Share Your Fears

Even though he is unable to admit it, Paul fears at some level that Molly and the other people he loves might value or love him less if he earned less money. He also fears that he might not be able to keep up with the demands of his jobs as he ages. Molly feels sad and frustrated because her dad seems to have missed the boat in terms of loving his work and money more than his family. Now that she's going to have a child, she's afraid that money issues are going to cause tensions between her and her dad—and possibly between her husband and her dad.

Paul is not self-aware enough to be in touch with his fears and he is not willing to share any vulnerable feelings with Molly. He wants his daughter to look up to him like a heroic Superman. He wants to be a "he-man" instead of a "hu-man" in her eyes. Fortunately, though, as he answers the questions, Molly is able to figure out what he fears: losing people's love and being less successful in the future than he is now. Above all, he seems to fear the physical and mental declines of aging, which might explain why he clings so desperately to his work.

★ Step 4: Propose a Plan

Molly lets her dad know that she wanted more time with him as she was growing up. She does this in a way that does not make him feel guilty. What's the point of a guilt trip when he can't undo the past? Instead of focusing on the past, she asks for two changes that he can make in the present. First, she tells him that she wants to spend more time alone with him and to have more conversations about things other than work. Second, she asks if he is willing to set aside time to have several long talks with her about his role as a grandfather. Paul agrees to both requests. She uses the questions in "Who Is This Man: Childhood, Values, and Friendship" to get to know her father as someone other than a man who is very focused on status, career, and money.

This first round of questions has set the stage for more detailed conversations in the near future about his role in the baby's life. In those future talks, Molly plans to ask Paul to agree not to substantial amounts of money on his grandchild without first checking it out with Molly and her husband. Of course, she will have to be specific about what she means by "substantial." She will also explain why she would like him to spend more time and less money on his grandchild. This will help him feel valued, not for his money, but for himself.

There are several take-home messages here for fathers and daughters in families where the dad seems to have focused more on work and money than on relationships. First, finding out why and how her father came to place such a high value on money and success can soften the daughter's negative views of him. As you can see from the fathers' and daughters' comments at the end of this chapter, some daughters end up feeling sorry for their workaholic dads, instead of feeling angry at them. Second, asking her dad questions about aspects of his life other than work and money can reveal a side of him that she has not seen before now.

Who Is This Man?

Quiz 4: Childhood, Values, and Friendship

Family

1   Who is (or was) your favorite relative? Why?
2   What do you like and dislike about each of your parents?
3   How are you like and unlike each of your parents?
4   What are three of your favorite childhood memories?
5   How did each of your parents show they loved you?
6   What did you get too little of and too much of from each of your parents?
7   How are you and your siblings alike and different? Why do you think that is?
8   What is something you wish—or would have wished—for your father? Your mother?
9   Other than a relative, what people meant a lot to you as a child and a teenager?
10 What was your best and your worst birthday while you were growing up?

Values

11 What is one of the books, movies or songs that means the most to you? Why?
12 If you could afford it, what would you buy or do?
13 What do you wish you had more of or less of? Why?
14 How do you define yourself politically?
15 If you could change two laws, what would they be?
16 What would bring you the greatest joy during the next few years?

Friendships

17 What are four traits you look for in a friend?
18 Who is your best male friend and what sets him apart from other men?
19 What is some of the best advice a friend ever gave you?
20 What have friends done that hurt you the most, and how did you deal with that?
21 What do your friends like the most and the least about you?
22 What are some of the best things your friends have ever done for you?
23 How have your friendships changed since you were my age?

Will It Be Worth It?

Will it be worth it to have long, private father-daughter conversations about the questions in this chapter? Whatever else happens, the payoff for the daughter is a more complete understanding of who her father is as a person, not just as her father. And the payoff for the dad is knowing that his daughter cares enough about him to want to know more about his life.

> "My dad told me that if he could do it all again, he wouldn't work for a big corporation and make all this money. All these years I thought he loved his work and that it was just normal for dads never to be at home. I didn't realize it bothered him to be away from me so much. As successful and well known as he is, I'm stunned."
>
> "I've never liked how obsessed he is about money. And he'd get upset with mom for spending too much. She'd laugh and brush

him off. So we three girls never took him seriously. After he told me about his poor childhood, I felt a pang of guilt thinking about how selfish the four of us girls must have seemed to him."

"I was totally shocked to find out that the reason he had gone to a lower paying job was to spend more time with us kids when we were young."

"Growing up, I just assumed he didn't want to be around us much because he was away a lot. I was stunned when he said he used to miss me a lot while he was away at sea and that looking at my picture made him tranquil. Suddenly I felt bad about myself for thinking of him as an unemotional person."

"It was hard to him to talk about himself. He kept insisting that I already know him, which I don't. He kept wanting to stop talking and told me to go to my mom to answer the questions. I kept pressing."

"This is the first time I've seen my dad as somewhat vulnerable. He's so successful at everything; but answering my questions made him incredibly nervous."

"I learned how trapped my father feels in his role as the only provider. In our community and our family, there's a mythology that follows him around because of all his success. Yet he said to me, 'I'm not as good as the public thinks I am.'"

"It was painful for him to talk about his father. He even asked me for advice. I actually reached over to him and said it was ok to talk to me about it. It was such a weird moment, me reaching out to help him."

"I realize that my dad was a victim of vicious cycles in his own family. I found myself excusing the fact that he has pretty much stumbled through fatherhood."

"The thing that glaringly stood out for me was that my dad still seems to trying to prove to his father that he's a big success—even though his dad has been dead for years."

"The most awkward part was when he said he wished I'd talk to him more and tell him what's going on in my head. This really bothered me because it forced me to acknowledge my faults in our relationship."

"I realize that I've been wanting to see him as perfect because he's so damn successful. But after he told me about his mistakes and failures at work, I felt closer to him and felt more comfortable sharing my fears and failures with him."

"The best thing was when we finished talking, he gave a big sigh and said he'd been really nervous. 'I was really scared to answer some of your questions. I mean, we never really talk about anything meaningful.'"

"It was very moving when my dad said the nicest gift I ever gave him was deciding finally that I want to take time to get to know him by asking him these questions."

In closing, keep in mind that many fathers and daughters are reluctant to discuss the financial issues that are straining their relationship. This is normal. But if you are making excuses for why you are not ready yet to address these problems, remember the old adage: "If you do what you've always done, you'll get what you always got." In future chapters we will explore other stressful situations involving money—issues that arise after the parents divorce or when the father is in the late stages of his life.

Reference List

(1) Robson D. This one's for dad. SportsWorld.com August 31, 2015:1–2.

(2) Callahan M. Lady Gaga gives 50 percent of her earnings to her father. *New York Post*, November 20, 2011.

(3) Cuccinello H. From Taylor Swift to Katrina Lake: America's richest self-made women under 40. *Forbes,* June 4, 2019.

(4) Caputo R. Adult daughters as parental caregivers. *Journal of Economic Issues* 2002;23:83–97.

(5) Coontz S. *History of marriage.* New York: Penguin; 2007.

(6) BLS. *Highlights of women's earnings in 2017.* Washington, DC: Bureau of Labor Statistics: U.S. Dept. of Labor; 2018.

(7) Parker K, Stepler R. *Americans see men as the financial providers.* Washington, DC: Pew Research Center; 2017.

(8) Close M, Heggeness M. Manning up and womaning down, June 6, 2018. Washington, DC: Census Bureau; 2019. Report No.: WP2018-20.

(9) Lino M, et al. *Expenditures on children by families, 2015.* Washington, DC: U.S. Department of Agriculture; 2017.

(10) Harrington B, Fraone J, Lee J, Levey L. *The new millenial dad: Understanding the paradox of today's fathers.* Boston, MA: Boston College Center for Work & Family; 2016.

(11) Livington G. Dads say they spend too little time with their children. Washington, DC: Pew Research Center; 2018. Report No.: January 8, 2018.

(12) Parker K, Livingston G. *Seven facts about American dads.* Washington, DC: Pew Research Center; 2017.

(13) Aumann K, Galinsky E, Mator K. *The new male mystique.* New York: Families and Work Institute; 2011.

(14) Patten E. *How parents blance work and family life when both work.* Washington, DC: Pew Research Center; 2015. Report No.: November 4.

(15) Pew Research Center. *Raising kids and running a household: How working parents share the load.* Washington, DC: Pew Research Center; 2015.

(16) Bianchi S, Sayer L, Milkie M, Robinson J. Housework: Who did or does or will do it and how much does it matter? *Social Forces* 2012;91:55–61.

(17) Connelly R, Kimmel J. If you're happy and you know it: How do mothers and fathers in the U.S. really feel about caring for their children. *Feminist Economics* 2015;21:1–34.

(18) Raley S, Bianchi S, Wang W. When do fathers care? Mother' economic contribution and fathers' involvement in child care. *American Journal of Sociology* 2012;117:1422–1459.

(19) Mahoney S. *In supermarkets, dads now top shoppers.* New York: Marketing Daily; June 12, 2012.

(20) Fikes D. *Shifting toward a shared grocery shopper paradigm.* New York: Food Marketing Institute; 2017.

(21) Kuo P, Volling B, Gonzalez R. Gender role beliefs, work-family conflict and father involvement after the birth of a second child. *Journal of Men & Masculinities* 2018;19:243–256.

(22) Horowitz J. *Who does more at home work when both parents work?* New York: Pew Research Center; 2015. Report No.: November 5.

(23) Barnes M. Gender differentiation in paid and unpaid work during the transition to parenthood. *Sociology Compass* 2015;23:348–364.

(24) B.L.S. *Employment characteristics of families: 2018.* Washington, DC: Bureau of Labor Statistics: USDL 190666; 2019.

(25) Chesley N, Flood S. Signs of change? At-home and breadwinner parents' housework and child-care time. *Journal of Marriage and Family* 2017; 79:511–534.

(26) Seaver M. The national average cost of a wedding is $33,391. theknot.com; 2019.

(27) Cha Y. Reinforcing separate spheres: The affect of spousal overwork on men's and women's employment in dual earner households. *American Sociological Review* 2010;6:6–7.

(28) Cha Y, Weeden K. Overwork and the slow convergence in gender gap in wages. *American Sociological Review* 2014;79:457–484.

(29) Glass J, Andersson M, Simon R. Parenthood and happiness: Effects of work-family reconciliation policies in 22 OECD countries. *American Journal of Sociology* 2016;122:886–929.

(30) Weeden K, Cha Y, Bucca M. Long work hours, part time work and trends in the gender gap in pay. *Russell Sage Foundation Journal of Social Sciences* 2016;2:71–102.

(31) B.L.S. *Time spent in primary activities by married mothers and fathers by employment status: 2007–2010.* Washington, DC: Bureau of Labor Statistics; 2015.

(32) Rauch J. *The happiness curve: Why life gets better after midlife.* New York: Green Tree; 2019.

(33) Kochanek K. Deaths: Final data for 2017. *National Vital Statistics Reports* 2019;68:1–16.

Chapter 3

Romantic Relationships, Sex, and Lifestyles

"Why not go out on a limb? Isn't that where the fruit is?"

Anonymous

If you are like most fathers and daughters, the daughter's romantic relationships, sexual behavior, and other lifestyle issues have strained your relationship somewhere along the line. Talking about these things often make fathers and daughters feel they are going out on a limb because the topics are so personal. But if we won't take the risk of going out on that limb, we cannot reap the benefits that come from resolving the lifestyle issues that stress the father-daughter relationship.

Some of these tensions over lifestyle issues start in the daughter's late teenage years: drinking, smoking, using recreational drugs, and having sex. Other issues appear later in her life: living with her romantic partner without being married, coming out as a member of the LGBTQ community, marrying or having children with someone of a different race, marrying too young or never marrying at all, choosing never to have children, or having children as an unmarried woman or as a member of the LBGTQ community.

Conflict over lifestyle differences, of course, works both ways. Sometimes father-daughter relationships suffer because the daughter is unwilling to accept her dad's lifestyle choices. For example, after her parents separate, she might strongly disapprove of her dad's choices in women—especially the woman he marries. Or she might distance herself from him because she disapproves of his having another child in the new marriage. Just because the daughter is younger than her dad does not mean she is more tolerant or open-minded about his lifestyle choices than he is about hers.

As we will see at the end of this chapter, these conflicts over lifestyles and values might begin with arguments or heated discussions about politics. Many of our political views reflect our deepest feelings about lifestyle issues such as marriage for same-sex couples, terminating unwanted pregnancies, legalizing marijuana, providing insurance coverage for contraceptives, or funding medical facilities that provide contraceptives and abortion services. Depending on how these political differences are handled, they can do serious and long-lasting damage to father-daughter bonds.

Famous Daughters and Their Fathers: The Daughter's Romantic Life

Lindsey Vonn, age 36, gold-medal Olympic skier, four World Cup Championships, retired in 2019

Lindsey Vonn's father, Alan Kildow, was a former ski champion who taught her to ski when she was three and coached her throughout childhood. Against her father's wishes, at the age of 22 she married a fellow Olympic skier. They had met when she was only 17. He was nine years her senior. Her husband became her coach and manager. Consequently, Lindsey and her father became estranged. Four years later, when she and her husband divorced, she reached out to her dad and they eventually reconciled.[4]

Megan Rapinoe, age 33, world-famous soccer player, winner of two World Cup Soccer Championships, and Sue Byrd, age 38, world famous basketball player, Olympic gold medalist

Megan and Sue came out as lesbians to their parents when they were in college, though the two women did not meet until years later. Although politically conservative dads are generally opposed to same-sex relationships,[5,6] this was not the case for Megan's dad, who does not share her liberal political views. Megan's dad, Jim, and Sue's dad, Herschel, were both supportive of their daughters. Megan has been a national spokesperson for LGBTQ rights since her early 20s. In media interviews, Jim has said he is proud of the woman, the athlete, and the leader she has become. The two women live together in Seattle and were the first gay couple to appear on the cover of *ESPN* magazine naked.[7] Megan also appeared in the *Sports Illustrated* swimsuit edition.[9,10,11]

Privacy vs. Lies and Deception

No matter how old they are, some daughters believe it is inappropriate or weird to talk to their dads about anything having to do with their personal lives. This is unfortunate for a number of reasons. First, the daughter is depriving herself of guidance that would probably enrich her life. Second, she is depriving herself of the comfort that her father could offer during the hard times. Whether she is going through a break-up or a divorce, dealing with drinking or drug abuse, or dealing with her own children's struggles, her father cannot comfort her if she is keeping him in the dark. Third, when daughters try to keep their fathers from finding out anything about their personal lives, they inevitably end up deceiving or outright lying to them. The lies and deceptions may be relatively small and harmless in the beginning. But if this unhealthy pattern continues, the daughter can wind up habitually lying to her father about her personal life. And when she deceives and lies to her dad, she is presenting a false, phony image of herself to someone who loves her—her father.

Many daughters and fathers would be more comfortable discussing their personal lives and lifestyle issues if they understood that this does not mean giving up their privacy. Being honest does not mean disclosing very private or terribly embarrassing details about our lives. In fact, we are routinely honest with close friends without violating anyone's privacy. For example, we find ways to let close friends know that we are sexually active or that our marriage is in trouble without necessarily providing them with any details that would violate anyone's privacy—or that would embarrass the listener. But we do not lie to close friends about these matters by deceiving them into believing that we have never had sex or that our marriage is blissful.

Some of us try to justify our lies and deception by telling ourselves: "I'm not lying, I'm just protecting my privacy. Besides, fathers and daughters shouldn't tell each other everything about their lives." True, privacy is a good thing. We should respect it. For example, we should not invade other people's privacy by reading their emails, eavesdropping on their conversations, rummaging through their belongings, or barging into an occupied bathroom without knocking first. But protecting our privacy does not mean deceiving or lying to each other. Privacy does not mean pretending to be someone other than who we are or pretending to hold beliefs that we do not hold. A simple test is this: do you feel guilty or uneasy about what you are withholding from the other person? If you do, then you have probably crossed the line from privacy to dishonesty. And that's a bad position to put yourself in.

More importantly, deceiving the other person reflects a deeper rift. When we deceive people, we are usually afraid that they will love us less if we let them see who we really are and what we really believe. We feel that we have to hide the "real me" in order to be loved or liked. Especially with family members, we should be asking ourselves: Why am I so afraid to tell this person who I really am and what I really believe? Exactly what am I afraid I might lose if this person discovers the real me—love, respect, financial support? How much longer can I go on pretending? The point is that maintaining our privacy and respecting one another's privacy do not create distance or troubles between people. But deception and dishonesty do.

What about secrecy? Is that a form of lying and deception? Is there any harm done when fathers and daughters keep secrets from each other? The secrets we are referring to here occur in the family network when certain members intentionally hide information from some members and share that information with others. What is important is not the actual content of the secret, but the *reason* for creating the secret in the first place. For example, the daughter confides in her mother that she and her boyfriend are living together. The two women keep this secret from the father. Or the father confides in one of his daughters that he and her mother are probably heading toward divorce, but they keep this a secret from the other daughter. Secrets like these are likely to be damaging if the truth ever comes out.

The point is that in a family, when we choose to exclude someone from a secret, that person is likely to end up feeling hurt, or unwanted, or perhaps even less loved. The hurtful message is: I do not trust you as much or do not feel as close to you as I do to the person I shared my secret with. The excluded person often feels like an outsider, an outcast, or an unwelcomed intruder. Generally speaking, daughters keep more secrets from their fathers than from their mothers. Dad is more likely than mom to be treated like the outsider. When they feel the need to keep secrets from one another, daughters and fathers should ask themselves: Why do I feel the need to keep this information secret from some family members and not others? What do I fear might happen if I share this information with the person I am excluding?

The other risk with secrets is that, over the years, the harmless little secrets over insignificant things sometimes morph into much bigger secrets. For example, a younger daughter and her mom may not let dad in on their little secrets: the daughter got into trouble at school or she lost her brand-new cellphone, even though they told dad it was stolen.

This pattern of secrecy may end up excluding the father from far more important information later in his daughter's life.

Consider Fred and his young adult daughter, Rose, who both claim they are not lying to each other. They both feel they are simply doing what has to be done to keep the peace. Fred has gone to great lengths over the years to hide the truth from Rose: he had a son with another woman before he met Rose's mother. Then he involved Rose's mother in the cover-up by getting her to agree never to divulge his secret. This is not a matter of privacy, especially since his son knows about Rose but Rose does not know about her half-brother. True, he did not outright lie to his daughter. But he intentionally hid the truth. If Rose ever discovers the truth, she is not likely to appreciate the fact that her father has deceived her all these years. With trust eroded, from then on, she might wonder: what else is my dad hiding from me? Why didn't he trust me enough to tell me the truth once I was mature enough to understand?

Though her secret is less serious, Rose is not being honest either. She has been deceiving her father for at least a decade. He is a very religious man who enjoys having her go to every religious service with him whenever she comes home to visit. She intentionally says things to her dad that lead him to believe she goes to services regularly and is actively involved in her church back home. Now that she is engaged, her dad is expecting her to have a religious church wedding. The truth is that Rose has not had anything to do with any religion for at least 10 years. She definitely does not want a religious ceremony, let alone get married in a church. What started out as a relatively harmless white lie has morphed into something much more complicated.

The point is that fathers and daughters can be honest about their lifestyles and their values without giving up their privacy. They do not need to resort to secrecy, lies, or deception in order to maintain their privacy, as we will see throughout this chapter.

Update Your Records: What Does Dad Believe?

As discussed in earlier chapters, the second step in addressing father-daughter troubles is for the daughter to discover more about her father. By asking him a series of questions about his life and carefully exploring his answers, a daughter learns how her dad came to hold certain values and beliefs that relate to the current obstacle facing them.

Especially when it comes to sex and other lifestyle issues, it is extremely important that fathers and daughters get an update on how each of them *currently* feels about these issues. Fathers' beliefs and concerns about their daughter's lifestyle generally become more liberal after she finishes high school, moves out of her parents' home, and has the legal status of an adult. But if daughters have not kept up to date with their dad's beliefs on lifestyle issues, they may be making assumptions about him that are creating unnecessary tension between them. For example, the father who disapproved of his daughter drinking or having sex as a teenager may be perfectly comfortable with her drinking and having sex as a young adult.

This is not to say you should count on the fact that all fathers and daughters will become more accepting or more open-minded as they age. Indeed, some people change in the opposite direction with age, becoming more judgmental and more socially, politically, or religiously conservative. The point is that the two of you need to update your records to be sure you are not being held back by outdated, false assumptions about one another's beliefs and values. We turn our attention now to some of the lifestyle situations that often create tension between fathers and daughters.

Drinking, Smoking, and Recreational Drugs

During adolescence, most daughters are already making lifestyle choices in regard to drinking, smoking and using marijuana. Understandably, most parents strongly disapprove of their teenage children smoking, drinking, or using drugs. Teenagers expect their parents to disapprove of this behavior. But once a daughter becomes a young adult, disagreements about drinking, smoking or drug use can create a more serious rift between her and her dad.

Consider the situation facing Alia and her father, Geoff. Alia has been smoking daily and drinking occasionally since she was in high school. Now that she has finished her education and is working, she and her best friend share an apartment. Whenever her dad plans to drop by, she and her roommate go through their apartment hiding any evidence that they smoke and drink. They have their routine down: take the beer out of the fridge, hide the wine glasses, stash all the alcohol in the back of the linen closet, spray a little room deodorizer to cover the smoke smell. By time her dad arrives, Alia is already a little on edge. She tries to limit the time he spends at her apartment so he has less chance to find traces of the evidence.

Her dad is adamantly against smoking and drinking given his religious beliefs and his upbringing. His younger brother died from lung cancer from heavy smoking. Over the past year, Geoff has been making many more negative comments to Alia about people who drink or smoke. Recently he asked her outright if she smoked, commenting that her clothes "smelled funny." She avoided answering by making a joke of it. More uncomfortable still, even though she is well past the age of 21, at several social events with her parents where alcohol was being served, she told the server in front of her dad, "No, thanks, I don't drink."

Deceiving and lying to her dad are becoming harder and making her more uncomfortable around him. She has also recently developed a smoker's cough. When her dad comments on it, she tells him that she probably has allergies—though, as he points out, she never had allergies as a child that caused any coughing. Sometimes he gives her very short notice before he drops by for a visit. That makes it harder for her to get rid of the evidence before he shows up. She worries that he is eventually going to discover the truth by accident. This will definitely add fuel to the fire.

As Alia puts it, "If I tell dad the truth, he will feel that I've betrayed his trust. I've been lying to him for so long. We've never really had any major issues between us. I'm afraid he won't trust me anymore if I fess up. But I sort of resent him for putting me in this situation. Almost everyone my age drinks, and so do most people in his generation. He should be relieved that I don't use drugs. I know I can't defend smoking to him. I can't even defend it to myself. I need to quit. But the drinking? No, I don't feel guilty about that and I don't plan to give that up. I'm not an alcoholic. I don't get drunk. It's almost as if dad is giving me no choice but to keep lying to him."

★ Step 1: Consider the Research

As we have seen in earlier chapters, the first step in reducing conflict is for both of you to get the research facts and accurate statistics. These facts will help you put your own situation into perspective by seeing where you stand compared to most other Americans. Taking these quizzes will also help you compare the similarities and differences in what each of you believe about the lifestyles of most Americans today. You might discover that you are both far off the mark in terms of what you know about the lifestyle choices that most American daughters are now making.

At the outset, fathers and daughters have to be sure they are not confusing drinking problems with alcoholism. The following list describes the symptoms of alcohol abuse disorders, otherwise known as alcoholism. Like any other drug addiction, addiction to alcohol cannot be resolved through family discussions. To be clear, the following advice is not applicable when the drinker is an alcoholic. Like any other drug addiction, combatting alcoholism requires professional help from mental health and medical professionals.

What Are the Symptoms of Alcoholism?[1]

Are you or is anyone else in your family an alcoholic? According to the *Diagnostic and Statistical Manual of Mental Disorders,* people have an alcohol abuse disorder if they have exhibited any two of these behaviors during the past 12 months:

- Had times when you drank more or longer that you intended?
- More than once wanted to cut down or stop but couldn't?
- Spent a lot of time drinking or being sick afterwards?
- Experience craving, a strong need, or urge to drink?
- Found that drinking often interfered with taking care of your home or family or caused job or school problems?
- Continued to drink even though it was causing trouble with your family or friends?
- Given up or cut back on activities that were interesting or pleasurable in order to drink?
- More than once gotten into situations while drinking that increased your chances of getting hurt (having unsafe sex, driving, using machinery, walking in a dangerous area)?
- Continued to drink even though it was making you feel depressed or anxious or adding to another health problem?
- Had to drink much more than you once did to get the effect you want?
- When the effects of alcohol were wearing off, had withdrawal symptoms such as trouble sleeping, shakiness, irritability, anxiety, depression, restlessness, nausea, or sweating?

_____ Your score

Since Alia is not an alcoholic, the first step is for her and her dad to take the following quiz on drinking, smoking, and using drugs. This sets the stage for discussing the specific situation that is creating tension between them.

What Do You Think?

Quiz 4: Drinking, Smoking, and Drugs

What do you think is true for most Americans today?

1   Daughters living in rural areas are less likely to drink or use drugs than daughters living in urban areas.
2   College-educated daughters are less likely to drink than less educated daughters.
3   Daughters are less likely to smoke than their mothers and their fathers.
4   College-educated daughters are less likely to smoke than less educated daughters.
5   Daughters with wealthy, well-educated parents are the least likely to drink or use drugs.
6   Women are more likely than men to use and become addicted to opioids.
7   Seventy percent of Americans drink.
8   Sixty percent of daughters have had a drink before age 18.
9   Thirty percent of daughters have engaged in binge drinking before the age of 20.
10 Forty-five percent of daughters have gotten drunk by time they graduate from high school.
11 Fifty percent of daughters have tried marijuana before the age of 21.
12 Thirteen percent of daughters vape and 15% smoke cigarettes.

_____ Your Score

How did your beliefs align with reality? All of the statements are true except one, two, and five. Daughters and sons in rural areas are *not* more or less likely to drink or use drugs than their peers in more urban areas. College students are *more* likely to drink than people their age who are not in college. Likewise, teenagers and young adults with wealthy, well-educated parents are *more* likely to drink and use recreational drugs than their peers from less-wealthy homes.[16,17,18,19,20]

★ Step 2: Don't Make Assumptions

In the second step, Alia spends a few hours with her dad asking him questions about his beliefs on drinking, smoking, or using recreational drugs. The goal is simply to find out how his beliefs developed and why he is so opposed to her drinking or smoking. She uses the following questions to move the conversation forward. Alia and Geoff are both uncomfortable having this conversation. He is uncomfortable because he senses that the religious gap between him and his daughter is probably larger than he realized. And she is uneasy because she knows that she has been lying to her father for years about drinking and smoking.

Who Is This Man?

Quiz 5: Smoking, Drinking, and Drugs

1 How have your opinions on drinking or smoking changed over the years?
2 How did you first form your opinions?
3 What do you fear might happen if I drink occasionally at social events?
4 How responsible do you feel about the choices your adult children make about smoking or drinking or using marijuana?
5 Do you feel somehow that you have failed as a parent if your adult children smoke, drink, or use recreational drugs?
6 What should a dad do if he finds out his teenage daughter smokes or drinks? What if she is in college or is older than 18?
7 When you were younger, how did your parents react when you made decisions about your personal life that they disapproved of?
8 Have you ever had a friend who smokes or drinks? How did you overlook their habit and manage to still have a good relationship with them?
9 Has anyone ever rejected or criticized you because you don't smoke or drink? How did that make you feel? Do you think the way they treated you was kind or fair?
10 If you had to rank behavior that you most disapprove of, how would you rank smoking, drinking, and using marijuana? Why?

★ Step 3: Identify and Share Your Fears

In these initial conversations with her dad, Alia learns more about his fears and feelings about drinking and smoking. Geoff fears that, if his daughter smokes and drinks, she is eventually going to turn her back on all of their family's religious beliefs. He also fears that drinking and smoking will bring her into closer contact with the "wrong kind" of people—people whose personal lifestyles and values will lead her down the "wrong path." He is also making a number of negative and unfounded assumptions about people who drink. For example, he tells Alia that young adults who drink almost always end up as alcoholics later in life. He also mentions that he had a cousin who was an alcoholic. He fears that alcoholism is a disease that runs in the family.

Alia's fears are very different from her dad's. She fears that her dad will respect her less if she tells him the truth. She also fears that she will lose his trust. Since she has lied to him about smoking and drinking for so long, he might not trust what she tells him from here on. She also worries that he will see her as someone who has poor judgment in other areas of her life, just because she smokes and drinks. In fact, though, she shares many of his views on other lifestyle issues.

★ Step 4: Propose a Plan

Alia begins by talking with her dad about the many lifestyle beliefs they share in common—for example, couples not living together before marriage. She also lets him know how much she appreciates many of the values that he instilled in her. By doing this, she is reassuring him that they share a lot in common—especially on lifestyle issues that are more important than smoking or drinking.

Her conversation with her dad might go something like this: "Dad, I know how much we both value honesty. So I want to be honest and let you know that I do occasionally drink, and I smoke. I was afraid to tell you because I don't want to lose your respect. I also didn't tell you because I feel bad about myself for smoking. I know I need to quit. Out of respect for your beliefs, I won't drink or smoke around you. But, for the sake of our relationship, I wanted you to hear this from me instead of finding out accidentally."

Now that she understands how many false assumptions he's making about people who smoke and drink, she can also help dispel his negative stereotypes. She can introduce him to some of her friends and allow him see for himself that they are not living "immoral" lives. She also suggests that he read some of the brochures from AA about alcoholism so he can see that occasional drinking is not a sign of alcoholism.

Geoff might respond in one of several ways. He might thank Alia for her honesty and, at some future point, realize that smoking and drinking are relatively minor concerns, compared to all of the other "disastrous" decisions his daughter might have made in her life by now. Hopefully he will focus more on what the two of them have in common and less on the two issues that separate them. He might never get to the point where her drinking and smoking don't bother him. But if he is wise, he will realize that harping on the topic will only create more stress. If the worst happens, and he starts criticizing or lecturing Alia, she can politely but firmly bring the conversation to an end with something along the lines: "Dad, we've been over this so many times. I know how you feel. I get it. I understand. It wasn't easy for me to be honest with you. I hoped you would appreciate that and let go of this. This is just one of things where we have to agree to disagree. This is not worth hurting each other over."

Regardless of how her dad responds, the upside is that she no longer has to feel guilty about deceiving him. As an added bonus, she frees herself from the burden of trying to hide the evidence in her apartment every time he comes to visit.

Sex: Facing Reality

As a daughter approaches early adulthood, and certainly well before she turns 30, she and her father have to acknowledge in some way that she has had sex. For most fathers, this is not shocking or upsetting news. Especially if their daughter is no longer in high school or has been dating the same man for some time, most fathers are fully aware that most young men and women have had sex by time they are in their early 20s—as was true in the father's generation as well.

Daughters have plenty of indirect ways of letting their parents know that they are having sex without having to make an official announcement. It might be as simple as leaving her birth control pills in an obvious place, like the bathroom counter, where her parents are bound to see them. Or she might make casual, off-handed comments that let the truth be known: For example, she might say: "The room that Al and I had was right on the beach." "The trip was okay, but Al and I didn't sleep well because our room was next to a noisy road."

Daughters can also get the message across in a light-hearted, joking way. For example, the daughter might find a way to interject the truth into a general conversation: "Sure, dad, George and I aren't doing anything except snuggling and holding hands until the day we get married." "Come on now, dad, I'm sure by time you were my age you were no innocent, naïve guy." Still another approach is the "I have a friend who—" technique. The daughter can always find a way to make a quick comment about her friend, along the lines: "You won't believe this, Dad, but my girlfriend's dad really believes that most women our age aren't having sex. What planet is he on?"

Still, there are fathers who feel that their daughter is not emotionally mature enough yet to be sexually involved with anyone, even though she may be well into her 20s. And there are dads who have no problem with the fact that their daughter is sexually active. What they object to is the man she is having sex with. And even when the father knows his daughter is sexually active, things can get strained between them when they have to deal with this reality in an "in your face" real life situation.

This is the dilemma facing Erin, her boyfriend Josh, and her dad Chuck. Even though she is no longer a teenager, Erin explains, "I've always been uncomfortable around Dad when there is anything even remotely related to my body or sex. A few years ago at a family outing, Dad commented that I looked good with the muscles I'd developed through weight training. I was wearing a bikini and suddenly I felt really embarrassed. The next day I realized that I'm the one who is uptight about anything having to do with my body. I assume Dad knows Josh and I are having sex since we've been dating over a year. But the subject has never really come up."

But now Erin and Josh are going to spend a night at her parent's house on their way to the mountains for the weekend. They want to share a bedroom since that have basically been living together for the past several months, even though they have separate apartments. Erin has also been wondering how to tell her parents that she plans to move in with Josh in a couple of months when her lease is up. As for the upcoming visit, from the comments her dad has made, it is clear he thinks Erin will be sleeping on the sleeper sofa in the den. So now what?

★ Step 1: Consider the Research

Erin and her dad are probably both already aware that the vast majority of young adults have had sex by time they are in their early 20s. Most couples also live together before they get married—if they get married. Still, some of the statistics in the lifestyle quiz might surprise some daughters and their dads.

What Do You Think?

Quiz 5: American Lifestyles and Sexual Behavior

What do you think is true for most Americans today?

1 By time they are 19, almost 50% of daughters have had sex.
2 Most girls are around 18 when they first have sex.
3 Daughters are waiting longer to have sex than women in their father's generation.
4 More than 75% of daughters have sex for the first time with a steady boyfriend or fiancé.
5 When teenagers accidentally become pregnant, about 30% terminate the pregnancy.
6 Almost 80% of sexually active teenagers and young adults use contraceptives.
7 Daughters from religious families are far less likely to have sex before marriage or to get pregnant as teenagers.
8 Eighty percent of married couples lived together beforehand.
9 Only about 10% of daughters are virgins when they get married.
10 A dad is as likely as his daughter to have had sex before marriage.

_____ Your Score

Which statements did you believe were true? The correct answer is all of them except number seven. Daughters from religious families are no less likely than other daughters to have sex before marriage or to get pregnant as teenagers.[21,22]

★ Step 2: Don't Make Assumptions

Just to be sure she is not confused about her dad's current beliefs, Erin takes time to explore the questions in the following quiz.

Who Is This Man?

Quiz 6: Love, Sex, and Relationships

1 How do you feel about couples living together or having children without being married? Why?

2 What were some of the best and worst experiences you had with women before you got married?

3 Other than with my mother, which romantic relationships had the greatest impact on you and how?

4 What do you wish you had known about women when you started dating?

5 How have your ideas about love, marriage and sex changed over the years?

6 What do you think it takes to make a good marriage?

7 What do you worry most about for me in terms of my relationships with men?

8 What are the biggest mistakes people make in choosing who to marry?

9 What do you wish you had known about sex and love when you started dating?

10 How did you know that mom was the right woman for you?

11 If you were a young woman, what traits would you look for in a man?

12 What are some of the signs that we're choosing the wrong person to marry?

13 What would you have done if your parents disliked the woman you were marrying?

14 What should a dad do if he doesn't like the man his daughter is in love with?
15 How are your views of love, sex, and marriage different from your parents' views?

★ Step 3: Identify and Share Your Fears

Erin first has to figure out why she is so uneasy about telling her dad outright that she wants to share a bedroom with Josh. What is she worried about? What does she fear her dad might say or do? She thinks back to what she learned about herself after the bikini incident. She reminds herself that she is generally more uncomfortable than her dad is about anything related to sex.

On the other hand, based on some of her dad's answers to the "Who Is This Man?" quiz, he might not feel too comfortable about her and Josh sharing a room in her parents' home. From his answers, it is clear that he doesn't care if unmarried couples live together. But some of his comments make her think he might not be so comfortable with her sharing a bedroom with her boyfriend in her dad's home.

★ Step 4: Propose a Plan

Since they live so far apart, Erin has to discuss this topic by phone. Otherwise, it would be better to discuss it in person. She begins the conversation with her parents by saying how much she and Josh are looking forward to the visit. Then she says there are several things she wants to find out more about—things like the plans for dinner and time of their arrival. This gives her a way to bring up the bedroom issue. Keeping things as simple as possible, she comments to her dad: "I hope you don't mind if Josh and I share the guest room." If she feels bold, she might add: "I'm sure you've figured out by now that Josh and I spend our nights together even though we're still in two apartments." To take the focus off anything sexual, she might jokingly say: "You wouldn't want me grouchy the next day with an aching back from that lumpy old sleeper sofa, right?"

Her parents might or might not have the same feelings about this situation. Keeping that in mind, Erin should not go behind her dad's back to try to get her mom's approval first. Their house is the home for both parents. If one of them is going to feel uncomfortable in their own home with Erin and Josh sharing a room, that person's feelings need to be respected. As it turns out, Erin's mom is okay with the idea. Her dad is not.

It might be tempting for the two women to gang up on Chuck and try to pressure him into doing what they want. This would be a mistake. First, her dad will be more likely to resent Josh and to feel tense during the visit if the two women force him into it. Second, he should not be forced into things that make him feel uncomfortable in his own home. Third, it is never good for the father-daughter bond when the mother and daughter gang up together against the dad. We will discuss this topic in the next chapter.

Since Chuck feels uncomfortable with the idea of Erin and her boyfriend sharing a bedroom while they are in his home, then he needs to say so. The key here is not to criticize the boyfriend. As Chuck explains to Erin, "Josh seems like a nice guy. I like seeing you so happy with him. What you two do in your own apartments isn't my business. But I don't feel comfortable having you two sleep together while you're here. Maybe it's because I don't know Josh that well and he's never been here before. Or maybe I'm just old-fashioned. Your mom and I never slept together in our parents' homes until we were engaged. Maybe next time you bring him home with you, I won't feel this way. But for this first visit, let's just stick with the lumpy old sofa plan."

This is not the answer Erin wanted. She is honest and tells her dad she is disappointed and hopes he will change his mind in the future. At the same time, she realizes that her dad is right about one thing: No matter how her mom feels, if her dad feels uncomfortable with the idea—or if he feels pressured into agreeing to it—then it will detract from the visit.

Erin has to rank her priorities. What outcomes are the most important to her in the short term and the long term? If her top priority is having her dad and boyfriend feel relaxed and get along well on this first visit, then she needs to let go of the idea of sharing the bedroom—at least for now. But if she feels so strongly about sharing a bedroom that she will be resentful and stressed during the visit, then she can book a room for them at a nearby motel. She also needs to consider the more important issue that lies ahead: telling her parents that she and Josh are moving in together. With that in mind, it is wiser to get her dad and Josh off to a good start on this first visit by letting her dad have his way about the bedroom.

Dad Dislikes His Daughter's "Man"

When it comes to smoking, drinking or sharing a bedroom with a boyfriend in their parents' home, daughters always have one surefire way to reduce the stress with their dad: just don't do those things when you are around your dad. It would be great if all fathers and daughters could sort out their troubles without having to resort to these "out of sight, out of mind" tactics. But that doesn't always happen.

As we all know though, the "out of sight, out of mind" tactic won't always work—or, it works, but only up to a certain point in time. Let's consider the situation where the dad does not like or approve of the man his daughter loves. Things have gone far beyond casual dating. The daughter is really serious about this guy and might very well end up marrying him. Understandably, a daughter wants her dad to like the man she loves. She hopes the two men get along well, even if they do not have much in common other than both of them loving her. She also wants her dad to like her boyfriend for another reason. To her, dad's approval means that he sees her as a mature, wise, intelligent woman—a woman with good judgment in men. When her dad disapproves of the boyfriend, it is more than simply disapproval of the man. It is disapproval of *her*. In her eyes, dad has judged her as immature, or foolish, or incompetent, or irrational for having made a bad choice. From her perspective, her father's disapproval of "her man" means he does not respect or trust her judgment. In short, there is a lot at stake when it comes to how dad feels about the man his daughter loves.

Most fathers are fully aware of these high stakes. The wise dad knows that he is going to have to ignore many of the boyfriend's minor imperfections—or at least not say anything to his daughter about those flaws. The wise dad thinks twice before he says anything negative to his daughter because her boyfriend has all those tattoos or because the guy spilled gravy all over the table at Thanksgiving.

But the wise dad sometimes finds himself trapped in a situation where he sees very serious problems that his daughter seems to be ignoring. Then what should he do, especially if she seems to be moving toward living with or marrying the man? Should dad speak up? If so, when? If not, why not? Are there circumstances where he should say nothing? But if he keeps his mouth shut, and things turn out badly for her, is he partly to blame—either in his own eyes or in hers?

Consider Margo and her father, Bruce, who have gotten along pretty well, except for the normal ups and downs of the teenage years. She is now in her last semester of college and has been dating Armand for almost a year. He is four years older than she is, has a good job, and has spent enough time around Margo's parents for Bruce to form some very strong opinions about him—unfortunately, not good ones. Bruce also knows from things Armand has said that he wants to start a family "soon." Bruce has never said anything negative to Margo about Armand. But recently things have changed. Margo has started hinting that they might get engaged soon. It was painfully clear to Margo from the expression on her dad's face and his tone of voice that he was not thrilled about the possibility of ending up with Armand as a son-in-law.

Bruce has stayed quiet for the past year because he figured—and hoped—things would fizzle out on their own. His concerns about Armand were there from the start. As Bruce explains, "Even though he's four years older than she is, Armand is a lot more emotionally immature than Margo. He's also very self-centered and bossy with her. I see why she's attracted to him. He's got a great job. He's handsome and athletic and has a good sense of humor. But he is really stuck on himself. Margo is so focused on pleasing him that I see her losing herself. And now she might base her future job decisions on where he lives. I wish she'd just live with him for a few years and see where that goes."

As Margo explains, "I'm really hurt and stunned that Dad isn't excited about the possibility of my marrying Armand. Dad must have known where things were headed since we've been dating for more than a year. He's never said a bad word to me about Armand. So why is he suddenly acting like this? I'm not a kid anymore. He should trust that I know what's best for me. Is he just upset because I'm not daddy's little girl anymore?"

The trouble between Margo and Bruce can also occur with much older daughters who are divorced and planning to remarry. Regardless of his daughter's age, a dad might disapprove of the man she loves—and wonder what, if anything, he should say about it. For example, he might feel his divorced daughter should wait longer before getting married again. Or he might be worried because her fiancé already has two children and a difficult, uncooperative ex-wife. The guy she loves comes with enough baggage to sink a ship. Or the dad might be wary because the man she loves is so much older than she is. The 15-year age gap might not seem like much of an obstacle now. But what about when his daughter is only 50, at the top of her game in her career, and in good health, and her hubby is 65, retired, and in need of considerable medical care? In short, dads can have serious concerns about the men in their daughters' lives no matter how old she is.

★ **Step 1: Consider the Research**

It would help Margo and other daughters understand their father's concerns if they considered the research and statistics on marriage, parenthood, and divorce. As the old saying goes, "love is blind." Dad can often see the man in his daughter's life more clearly and more realistically than she can. How closely do your beliefs about marriage, motherhood, and divorce align with reality?

What Do You Think?

Quiz 6: Marriage and Motherhood

What do you think is true for most Americans today?

1 Couples with children are less likely to divorce than those without children.
2 Very religious couples are half as likely to divorce than less religious couples.
3 Fifteen percent of women do not ever have children.
4 Fifty percent of women have their first child by the age of 30.
5 Forty percent of children are born to unmarried mothers.
6 Fifty percent of married women end up divorced.
7 Almost 20% of married adults are married to someone of a different race.
8 Roughly 50% of daughters are married by time they are 30.
9 Couples who marry in their early 20s are more likely to divorce than those who wait until they are closer to 30.
10 Second marriages are more likely to end in divorce than first marriages.
11 Almost half of all marriages are second marriages for one or both spouses.
12 About half of all Americans approve of couples living together without being married.

_____ Your Score

Which ones did you believe were true? The correct answer is: all of them, except the first two.[23,24,25,26]

★ Step 2: Don't Make Assumptions

Having considered the research facts, Margo is ready to explore her dad's history. Quiz #6 enables her to see how her dad came to have his particular beliefs about love and marriage. What led him to his current beliefs and how strongly does he feel about them?

★ Step 3: Identify and Share Your Fears

Once Margo has explored the "Who Is This Man?" questions with her dad, she has a better handle on why he feels the way he does about love and marriage. Now they have to share their fears and feelings with each other. Bruce needs to explain his feelings in terms of his fears for Margo. He needs to help her see that his concerns are centered on her. He also needs to reassure her that he is not trying to control her and that he respects her right to make her own decisions. More important still, he has to be careful not to come across as judging Armand as a "bad" person. He has to express his concerns without trashing the man she loves.

Bruce starts by saying, "I know how much you love Armand. And I see what attracts you to him. I just want to share some of my concerns with you and put a few things out there for you to think about. I worry that you might be rushing into this and that you might be happier in the long run if you waited. You seem so focused on his needs that you push your own needs off to the side a lot. I also worry that that you might accept a job that is not going to make you as happy as you might have been if you hadn't based your decision on where Armand lives. I've made plenty of mistakes and bad decisions with women. I'm just really trying to spare you from making the same mistakes I made."

Margo also needs to figure out what she fears and share those feelings with her dad. "I'm afraid you'll make Armand feel unwelcomed if we get married. Or maybe you'll say something that lets him know you never wanted him for a son-in-law. I'm also upset with you for not trusting my judgment. It feels like you're trying to control my life. I know what's good for me and what's not. You just have to trust me."

Bruce tries to stay calm, though he feels unfairly judged. "I do feel you have good judgment in those areas of your life where you have had enough experience to make good decisions. I mean, I trust your judgment about your career choice because in your four years at college you had several different summer internships and many different courses that helped you explore your interests. But there are some areas of your life where you have not had enough experience to make the best choices for yourself. And for all of us, me included, good judgment and good decisions depend a lot on how much experience we've had. I think getting married this young might be one of those areas. You haven't had the experience yet of starting your career or living on your own. You haven't had the experience of actually living with Armand. So I'd just feel less worried for you if you allowed yourself to have more of those experiences before you make a decision as serious as marriage."

★ **Step 4: Propose a Plan**

With their fears and feelings out in the open, Margo and Bruce can each offer ideas for ways to reduce the strain. To be clear, the goal here is not how Bruce can convince Margo not to marry Armand. The problem is that he does not know how to share his concerns in a way that will not drive her away. Unlike some fathers, Bruce understands that he cannot stop his daughter from marrying anyone she wants any time she wants. Giving her advice is a loving thing to do. But doing anything more than that is a surefire way to drive a wedge between him and Margo. He is also smart enough to realize that he is going to have to accept whatever decision she makes, even if he does not approve of it.

Bruce's main goal is to reduce the stress with his daughter. His other goal is to share his concerns in the least damaging way possible. He starts by asking her if they can spend some time together to talk about Armand. He promises not to bring the topic up again if Margo will just hear him out this one time. Then he promises that if things with Armand don't work out, he will never say things like: "I told you so. I warned you about him. You should have listened to me." So they talk. He lets her know how he feels without coming across as judgmental. He ends by suggesting that she and Armand live together for a year or so before making a decision about marriage. He ends with: "I'm not telling you what you should or shouldn't do. I'm just putting these ideas out there for you to think about."

Regardless of whether she ends up marrying Armand, this father-daughter conversation is beneficial. Why? Because if Margo gets married and it fails, Bruce will have a clear conscience. He did what he could to protect his daughter by speaking up. He will never have to blame himself for having failed as a dad in that regard. Margo benefits too, because she will never resent her dad for not speaking up. If she does marry Armand and things work out, she and her dad can still be proud of themselves for having the kind of bond where he felt free to share and she was willing to listen.

LGBTQ Daughters and Their Fathers

The advice offered throughout this book applies to daughters and fathers regardless of their sexual orientation. But LGBTQ daughters and their fathers face unique challenges. In some cases, the strain between them is happening because the dad is simply misinformed about LGBTQ relationships. Even the most well-intentioned father may need some educating. Of course, there are fathers who need a lot more than educating.

There are at least three questions that are too complex to be addressed in a small section of a book. First, how and when should a daughter tell her parents that she is not heterosexual? Second, how should parents react when they are told? Third, what can a daughter do if either parent rejects her after she comes out? Entire books have been devoted to answering these complicated, sensitive questions. Organizations such as PFLAG (pflag,org. Parents and Friends of Lesbians and Gays) also offer many resources for LGBTQ children of all ages and their parents.

Our focus here is how to deal with problems that occur well after the daughter has told her parents that she is gay. One of the most common stressors is telling her dad that she is going to marry and raise children with another woman. This situation can also drive a wedge between mothers and daughters. But, compared with women, men are generally more uneasy with gay and lesbian relationships and marriage for same-sex couples. So, the daughter's bond with her father is more likely to be tested and stressed than the bond with her mother.

So let's consider Kayla's situation with her dad, Andrew. Kayla came out to her parents five years ago. Neither of them seemed upset or even surprised. Since coming out, everything has seemed pretty much the same on the family front. But this might have been because she lived so far away and she never brought any of her partners home to meet her parents. During those years, she would occasionally mention that she and a girlfriend had gone to a party or had gone on a vacation together. She wasn't hiding the truth. It's just that her lifestyle was basically "out of sight, of mind" given the circumstances.

Recently though, things have started getting more uncomfortable between Kayla and her dad. Kayla and her partner, Rebecca, have moved in together after being together for several years. This happened when they were finally able to find good jobs in the same town—a town that is conveniently located only 30 minutes from where all of their parents live. Kayla recently mentioned to her parents that she and Rebecca are planning to get married sometime this year and to start a family soon afterwards. Although Kayla has not given her parents any details yet, they are hoping to each have a child through artificial insemination. Ideally, they want each of their children to be conceived from the same sperm donor so they will be biological half-siblings. In short, the "out of sight out of mind" strategy has come to a swift and sudden halt.

Whenever Kayla has talked to her parents about her plans, the conversations have been pretty brief and superficial. Without going into a lot of detail, she has talked in a matter-of-fact way to avoid making a big deal out of what lies ahead. Her parents have both met Rebecca briefly on several occasions. But because the two women did not live near their parents until recently, neither of Kayla's parents have had a chance to get to know Rebecca very well. Kayla's mom seems pretty relaxed about the whole thing. But her dad is a different story. So she knows she is going to have to talk to him—which is not something she is looking forward to.

Although Andrew never thought he had any bias toward the LGBTQ community, he is slowly realizing that he is uncomfortable with the idea of his daughter marrying and having children with a woman. With their being married and living so nearby, Andrew knows he will be expected to spend much more time with the two of them. And when they have children, he will definitely be expected to be an actively involved grandfather. Kayla's brother and his wife already have one child and are planning to have more. Andrew is a doting grandfather. Will he feel differently about Kayla's and Rebecca's children? If each of the women has a child through sperm donation, will he feel closer to Kayla's child? It's clear that Kayla's lifestyle is going to have much more of an impact on his life than it has up until now. So the question is: why does he feel so uneasy?

As Kayla puts it: "I think some of Dad's fears about my sexuality are starting to creep in. My brother tells me that Dad is having a hard time wrapping his head around the idea of my having kids with Rebecca. So that's making me wonder if dad is going to love my child as much as he loves my brother's child."

★ **Step 1: Consider the Research**

The first step for Kayla and Andrew is a reality check with the research on gay and lesbian couples. After taking the quiz, Andrew will at least be well enough informed to have a more rational conversation with

Kayla. The quiz might also help him get in touch with his fears and help him think about specific questions he needs to discuss with Kayla.

What Do You Think?

Quiz 7: LGBTQ Relationships

What do you think is true for most Americans today?

1 Nearly 25% of American daughters identify themselves as lesbians.[15]
2 Children raised by lesbian parents are just as well-adjusted emotionally, behaviorally, and psychologically as those raised by heterosexual parents.[3]
3 Roughly 60% of Americans are in favor of same-sex marriages.[5]
4 Of same-sex couples who live together, 60% are married.[5]
5 The public is generally more accepting of lesbians than of gay males.[2]
6 Lesbian mothers generally encounter less discrimination than gay fathers.
7 The most difficult years for most LGBTQ individuals are the adolescent years.[14]
8 Most lesbians come out to their friends or mother before they come out to their dad.
9 The vast majority of lesbians do not have emotional or psychological problems.[14]
10 Most gay and lesbian youth come out around the age of 14.[14]

_____ Your Score

What did you believe? All of the statements are true, except the first one. Even though the general public assumes that large numbers of Americans are not heterosexual, in fact only 3.8% of men and woman identify themselves as LGBTQ.[27] Most lesbian couples who are raising children together either became parents through sperm donation or had biological children in a prior heterosexual marriage. Although the majority of Americans are in favor of same-sex marriages, the general public disapproves more of gay men raising children than of lesbian couples doing so. Despite the disapproval their parents encounter, the children of gay men and lesbians are just as well-adjusted as the children of heterosexual parents. Given the hostility and discrimination they still face in society, lesbians are more likely than heterosexual women to become clinically depressed and to drink heavily. But in general lesbians are just as well-adjusted emotionally, socially and psychologically as heterosexual women, especially once they move beyond the teenage years where discrimination and rejection are the most intense.

★   Step 2: Don't Make Assumptions

Next Kayla sets time aside to carefully explore her father's beliefs and feelings about lesbians. Where did his beliefs come from? What is the source of his fears or worries about Kayla's plans to marry and have children with a woman?

Who Is This Man?

Quiz 7: LGBTQ Relationships

1   How do you feel about gay men or lesbians being allowed to marry? Why?
2   How many gay couples have you known who are raising children together?
3   Was there anything you noticed in those families that concerned you? If so, what?
4   How do you think children raised by heterosexual parents are different from kids raised by gay or lesbian couples?
5   How are your feelings or beliefs about gay families similar or different from those of your friends?
6   Have any of your feelings or beliefs about gay or lesbian couples changed over the years? If so, how and what caused the change?
7   How do you feel about heterosexual women having children through sperm donation? Do you feel any differently if the woman is gay?
8   What concerns do you have for children conceived through sperm donation?

★ Step 3: Identify and Share Your Fears

Taking the quiz helps Andrew identify some of his fears and feelings. Like the majority of Americans, he does not object to gay or lesbian marriage—in principle at least. His fear and anxiety mainly revolve around gay couples raising children together. Still, he is anxious when he thinks about how Kayla's lifestyle is going to affect his social interactions with people outside the family. Nobody he knows has gay or lesbian children—at least, not that he is aware of. How are the people in his social network going to react or interact with Kayla, her wife, and their children? Won't people wonder about the sperm donor who fathered his daughter's child? If they ask about the sperm donor, what is Andrew supposed to say? Is he even supposed to ask his daughter about the sperm donor? If so, when and how? He feels tense thinking about how awkward this is going to be as difficult situations like these unfold. He fears that all of this is going to strain things with Kayla over the coming years.

Kayla has similar fears, though from a different perspective. She fears that if her father is not fully on board with her marrying and having children, her close ties with him will deteriorate. They may eventually drift apart. She also fears that things with Rebecca will become complicated if her dad is really uptight around them and their future children. How will he handle their wedding? How will he handle the children's births? She tries to picture her dad at the hospital with them immediately after their babies are born. How well will he react? One thought leads to another, and none of them are happy ones.

★ Step 4: Propose a Plan

After Kayla and Andrew share their fears with one another, they need to focus on specific ways to reduce the strain. It is clear to both of them that his fears are mainly about Kayla and Rebecca raising children together. It is not that he disapproves of same sex marriage. His fears and discomfort are mainly rooted in his concerns for what he believes is best for children. But he is also anxious about how to handle the whole sperm donor situation.

Given her father's concerns, Kayla's first step is to hone in on some of her dad's false assumptions about children raised by lesbian couples. She explains to him that, according to decades of research on this question, children raised by gay or lesbian parents are just as well-adjusted as children raised by heterosexual parents. She walks him through some of specific research findings without sugar coating some of the unpleasant findings. The goal is to reassure her dad that she is not naïve about the challenges that lie ahead. Yes, the research does show that children and their LGBTQ parents face more challenges than heterosexual parents. For example, there are times when children with LGBTQ parents feel embarrassed around their friends or are teased or even bullied. But families have ways of working through this, including the use of children's storybooks specifically written for LGBTQ parents and their kids. Teachers are also more likely nowadays to recognize the needs of these children and to put a stop to bullying and teasing at school. And Kayla acknowledges to her dad that she and Rebecca know they are probably going to have to deal with discrimination, rejection, or ridicule. Then she reminds him that there are social, religious, and community groups and books to help families through this. Kayla also tries to reassure her dad by pointing out that society is more accepting than it was in his generation, especially for people in her age group. Just as society's attitudes about interracial marriages and biracial children have changed, attitudes toward LGBTQ families have also evolved. Then too, she reminds him that they will be raising their children in an urban area where attitudes tend to be more accepting.

As for the whole sperm donor issue, Kayla asks her dad to tell her more about his concerns. This must be hard for Dad, she thinks. And it is. But he manages to voice his worries: "What am I supposed to tell people if they ask about your child's father? Am I allowed to ask you questions about the sperm donor or is that prying? If you ever divorce, what happens to the kids in terms of custody? I mean, if you're the biological mom of one child and she's the biological mom of the other child, what happens to the children if your marriage ends?"

Because her dad has always had a good sense of humor, and because he enjoys reading children's stories to her brother's young child, Kayla decides to start with a light-hearted, child-centered approach. She shows him several children's books designed to answer young children's questions about conception through sperm donation. These books are designed not only for LGBTQ parents. Other books are designed specifically for kids being raised by two gay dads or two lesbian moms. As Kayla laughingly notes, "Well, you know dad, there are heterosexual men who have slow swimming 'tadpoles' and whose wives can only conceive through anonymous sperm donation. And their kids do fine and feel loved even though they don't have any of their dad's DNA—just like adopted kids or step-kids. It's not the sperm that counts. It's the love." She reassures her dad that they have thought ahead in terms of how and when to tell their children about their sperm donor fathers. And whatever explanations the two mothers offer, the grandparents can follow their lead. As for discussing anything about the future sperm donor with their parents, Kayla reassures her dad that all four grandparents will be privy to the same information. As little or as much as the two women eventually decide they want to share, they will share it equally with all four grandparents.

From there Kayla moves on to answer his questions about divorce and child custody. She is annoyed that he is thinking about the possibility of her getting divorced before she is even married. Wisely, she puts that feeling aside because she sees that his question stems from a loving concern for her future children. Having already read the child custody laws for same sex marriages in the state where she and Rebecca are married, she can answer her dad's questions calmly and confidently. Again, her objective is not to give him a lecture on child custody laws. Her goal is to reassure him that she and Rebecca are already taking their future children's well-being into account by becoming familiar with their state's child custody laws.

At the end of their conversation, Kayla addresses the less important matter: her dad's anxieties about how to handle social situations involving her, Rebecca, and, at some future point, their children. She can't answer some questions because there is no way to predict what kinds of social situations might make Andrew feel awkward over the coming years. But she does take two concrete steps to bring her and her dad closer. First, she lets her dad know that it is okay for him to be anxious about how he will handle those awkward situations in the future. In fact, she tells him that there are books for family members that offer specific ideas for how to handle those kinds of awkward moments. Second, she reassures him that when those situations pop up, the two of them will work together as a family team to figure out the best solutions. "I'm counting on you, Dad. Both Rebecca and I need you." This approach puts the emphasis on his importance, rather than emphasizing his anxieties.

Hopefully Andrew will realize that maintaining close ties with his daughter will bring him far more pleasure than criticizing or fretting about her life style. As we already discussed, when a father disapproves of his daughter's boyfriend or fiancé, he can express his concerns in ways that do not create a gap between them. The same holds true for a father who disapproves of his LGBTQ daughter's choices.

Political Differences and
Father-Daughter Stress

This chapter ends with political differences that can damage the father-daughter bond. Lifestyle issues are often at the root of the widening differences that have emerged between Democrats and Republicans in recent years. Especially after the election of Donald Trump as President in 2016, people's political party affiliations became an even stronger and clearer measure of their lifestyle values.[16–19] As the following quiz illustrates, Democrats and Republicans are further apart than ever on issues such as abortion, same sex marriage, and contraception.

Damage caused by political issues is evident in the situation confronting Autumn and her father, Kendal. They have both known since she was in college that they do not share the same views on many lifestyle issues, whether it's legalizing marijuana or allowing women to end unwanted pregnancies. But when she found out that her dad had voted for Donald Trump, the tensions escalated.

As Autumn explains, until the 2016 election, she and her dad generally avoided discussing social or political issues. But since then it has become harder to sidestep the issue. She realizes that the tension between her and her father is not just about who they voted for in 2016. It is about the profound differences in their values. She never expected he would take the extreme positions she was now witnessing. To complicate things even more, her two children are old enough now to understand some of the homophobic, racist, or sexist things that Grandpa says about people who are a lot like their parents' friends. "I'm always on the verge of exploding when he says these ridiculous or hateful things in front of the kids. How far is he going to take this? I could tolerate it if it was just me. But I'll be damned if I'm going to let him keep saying those kinds of things around my kids."

Kendal, too, is extremely frustrated, hurt, and annoyed. How can Autumn reject the values he instilled in her? How did she turn into such a leftist, liberal "nut case"? Why can't she see the damage that her liberal beliefs are having on her own children? Why is she so hardheaded and unwilling to listen to his opinions? Why won't she at least read the books or visit the websites he recommends to her? Why is she so angry and touchy?

The first step for Autumn and Kendal is to realize that their situation is not so unusual, by taking the following quiz. The differences between the social and lifestyle values of Democrats and Republicans is greater than ever before. And these differences have contributed to more strain on family ties.

What Do You Think?

Quiz 8: Political Parties and Lifestyle Issues

What do you believe is true for most Americans today?

1   Most parents and adult children have profoundly different political views.[2]
2   Compared with 10 years ago, adults are more likely now to disagree with their parents on politics.
3   Republicans are more likely than Democrats to disapprove of their children marrying someone of a different race, religion, or political persuasion.[6,8]
5   People over age 65 are twice as likely to disapprove of interracial marriage as adults under 30.[8]
6   College graduates are more likely than less-educated Americans to interact with people of a different race or sexual orientation.[8]
7   After the 2016 presidential election, family relationships became more strained by political differences.[12,13]
8   Republicans and Democrats are more likely than ever to have very different beliefs about social, religious, and lifestyle issues.[14]
9   Women in predominantly Republican states have fewer teenage pregnancies, lower divorce rates, and fewer children born out of wedlock than those in Democratic states.
10 Fathers whose first child is a girl are generally more supportive of liberal political policies that are designed to increase gender equality and to reduce violence.[15]

_____ Your Score

Which statements did you believe were true? All of the statements are true, except #1 and #9, which are false.

The good news for fathers and daughters is that most parents and their adult children have similar political views. They generally belong to the same political party and vote in similar ways. But there is also bad news. Since the 2016 presidential election, family members and friends have become more divided over politics.[28] For example, in a 2018 American Psychological Association national survey, nearly one-third of adults said that, since 2016, political differences have created turmoil in their family.[12] These arguments and bitter feelings, even if not openly discussed, sometimes escalate to the point that family members can no longer spend time together. In other words, father-daughter bonds are more likely nowadays to be strained by their political differences.

Many political arguments between family members revolve around lifestyle issues that are especially important to women; for example, easy access to contraceptives and health care and more acceptance of having children outside of marriage. Given this, it is worth noting that, despite Republicans' more conservative views, there are more teenage pregnancies, more out-of-wedlock births, and more divorces in Republican than in Democratic states. But the point is that, regardless of which state they live in, fathers are probably more likely to clash with their daughters than with their sons over political issues that have the greatest impact on women. And these are the kinds of political arguments that have become more intense since Trump eliminated policies that formerly benefitted women's health and reproductive freedom.

Obviously the four-step method isn't going to change a person's deeply held political beliefs, especially when those beliefs span a wide range of social and lifestyle issues. In fact, continuing to do battle with family members over extreme political differences does *not* increase the likelihood that anyone will adopt the other person's view.[2]

So where does this leave fathers and daughters like Autumn and Kendal? In part, the answer depends on how much damage is being done and how peacefully they can discuss their differences. If Autumn or her dad feel that discussing their political views might reduce the tensions between them, they should agree to abide by certain guidelines. First, they should only discuss one issue at a time. They should not talk about the views of either political party or of any candidate on a wide range of issues. Second, they must *never* go into these discussions expecting to change the other person's views. The only goal is to understand *why* each of them has those views. Third, try to find some common ground. For example, they may disagree on same-sex and interracial marriage, but they may agree that it's best for children to be raised in two-parent families instead of one-parent families.

On the other hand, Autumn or Kendal might decide that the best way to reduce the stress is to never discuss politics. Still, Autumn cannot allow her dad to continue making racist, sexist, or homophobic comments in front of her children. This is too important an issue for her to ignore. She explains to her dad that expressing his views on politics or other social issues around her children has to stop. She explains that she and her husband are raising their children to have very different values than those her dad holds. "I'm sure you'd agree with me, Dad, that it is up to the parents and not up to grandparents to decide these things." Without posing this as a threat, she can also explain that "if you enjoy having time with your grandkids, you will need to stop making those comments around them." Instead of making him feel he is being threatened or ordered around, this puts Kendal in the position of making the choice.

Whichever decision Autumn and Kendal make, their aim should be to reduce the animosity and tension between them. They should not be aiming to convert the other person to their own point of view. As a father or a daughter, we can respect the other's right to have his or her own opinions. To be clear, respecting does not mean agreeing or approving. That said, when a person's political comments cross the line in terms of violent, crude, or hateful talk, we may have no choice but to leave—whether that means leaving the Thanksgiving table or leaving each other alone by having limited contact for some period of time.

Will It Be Worth It?

Will it be worth it if you take the steps to discuss the lifestyle issues that are creating tension in your father-daughter relationship? Your discussions about sex, relationships and lifestyles are probably going to be a lot more uncomfortable than discussions about less personal topics like money. You *are* going out on a limb, which is scary. But, as you will see from these real daughters' comments and insights, going out on that limb was worth it.

Sad, But Insightful, Outcomes

"My dad was ruthless in criticizing my weight when I was growing up. He is overweight too. But I see now that's part of why I'm not comfortable with my sexuality even at my age."

"I wish dad had found ways to express his dislike of my boyfriends without being so hurtful and attacking. A lot of what Dad said turned out to be true. But the way he said things just drove a wedge between us. And the wedge is still there."

"My relationship with my father has always been volatile and angry. He is domineering and intimidating. I see now that's why I choose guys I can dominate. It makes me feel superior and gives me all the control."

Happy Insightful Outcomes

"I used to think of my dad as a prude. But after he told me about some of his young romantic relationships, I realized he wasn't just some uptight, bald guy with his head always stuck in a book. The odd thing is that I feel more relaxed now talking to him about my boyfriend."

"The weird thing is that Dad and I discovered that I'm the conservative one. I'm against abortion, premarital sex, and gay marriage. But he isn't. I was shocked, to say the least."

"My father is a quiet, shy man. He has never talked before about how he felt when he met my mom. But then, I had never asked him. While he was talking, I saw him as a young man falling in love. There was a tenderness in his voice I've never heard. Then he told me how scared he was to hold me when I was born and how he just cried and cried with relief because he was so worried because mom had already had several miscarriages."

"I wasn't looking forward to asking Dad questions about his sexual or romantic life. To tell the truth, I had two glasses of wine before we started talking to get myself relaxed. But given what he told me about his past with women before he met mom, I see him as a person who struggles through life as a man, and a husband—not just as my father."

"My dad told me about his first marriage—something my mother told me never to ask him about. But he was very open. And he said 'everyone needs to fumble around a little and make mistakes in order to figure out what they want and what makes them happy. You can't expect to get it right the first time—I certainly didn't.' His admitting his mistakes means I don't have to be perfect in his eyes. I ended up telling him the truth about why my marriage ended."

"I was surprised when he talked about being hurt by women when he was a young man. I don't think of him as vulnerable or fragile in any way. He's a fairly famous person in his field. Everyone is kind of intimidated by him. Until we talked, I had never heard him say he ever felt inadequate."

"I always felt uncomfortable talking to my dad about personal stuff. But after hearing his stories, I was surprised how easy it was to open up to him about the problems in my marriage."

"He told me how much he admired the way I dealt with having been raped as a teenager. We haven't talked about it since then because I've always thought he was ashamed of me. I was so relieved. I wish I'd told him years ago how I felt. It would have made me feel so much more comfortable around him."

"A few weeks ago my fiancé and I had an argument in front of my dad. Later that week Dad emailed me. He explained how my way of arguing with Sebastian could have been better. He wasn't mean. But he pointed out ways I attacked when I shouldn't have. He was really helpful. I think he felt comfortable giving me this advice because of the conversations we'd had doing those quizzes."

"I've always gone to my dad with questions about love. He's much more romantic than my mom. While he was answering the quiz questions, I realized that he is the one who helped me realize I was in a dead end relationship with a man I wasn't really in love with "My Dad is the one who talked with all us girls about sex, birth control, tampons and having our periods. At the time, I was a little embarrassed. But I realized in talking to him that he set the stage for our being able to talk openly about any topic from then on. I expect my future husband to do the same thing if we have a daughter."

Reference List

(1) A.P.A. *Diagnostic and statistical manual of mental disorders.* Washington, DC: American Psychiatric Association; 2013.

(2) Ojeda C, Hatemi P. Accounting for the child in the transmission of party identification. *American Sociological Review* 2015;80:1150–1174.

(3) Russell S, Fish J. Mental health in lesbian, gay, bisexual and transgender youth. *Annual Review of Clinical Psychology* 2016;12:465–487.

(4) Minutaglio R. Who is Lindsey Vonn? *Good Housekeeping,* January 12, 2018.

(5) Geiger A, Livingston G. Eight facts about love and marriage in America. Washington, DC: Pew Research Center; February 13, 2019:1–2.

(6) Iyenger S, Sood G, Lelkes Y. Affect, not ideology: A social identity perspectve on polarization. *Public Opinion Quarterly* 2012;76:405–431.

(7) Curtis C. 15 stunning images from ESPN's 2018 body issue. *ESPN, Body Issue,* June 25, 2018.

(8) Najle M, Jones R. *American democracy in crisis: The fate of pluralism in a divided nation*. Washington, DC: Public Relgion Research Institute; 2019.

(9) Voepel M. Ready to let you in. *ESPN.com*, July 20, 2017.

(10) Butterfield A. Megan Rappinoe's father couldn't be prouder. *The Daily Mail. com*, July 6, 2019:1–2.

(11) Sports Illustrated swimsuit edition. *Sports Illustrated*, May 2019.

(12) American Psychological Association. *Stress in America*. Washington, DC: American Psychological Association; 2018.

(13) Holand S, Silver B. *I think you're wrong but I'm listening*. Nashville, TN: Thomas Nelson; 2019.

(14) Hetherington M, Weiler J. *Authoritarianism and polarization in American politics*. New York: Cambridge University Press; 2009.

(15) Sharrow E. The first daughter effect: The impact of fathering daughters on men's preferences for gender equality policies. *Public Opinion Quarterly* 2018;82:493–523.

(16) ASAM. *Opioid addiction 2016: Facts and figures*. Rockville, MD: American Society of Addiction Medicine; 2017.

(17) Thompson A, et al. Time trends in smoking onset by sex and race among adolescents and young adults: Findings from the 2006–2013 national survey on drug use and health. *Nicotine & Tobacco Research* 2018;20:312–320.

(18) NIH. *Substance use in women*. Washington, DC: National Institutes of Health; 2018.

(19) Johnston L, et al. *Key findings on adolescent drug use*. Ann Arbor: Institute for Social Research, University of Michigan; 2017.

(20) Kann L, et al. *Youth risk behavior surveillance: 2017*. Atlanta, GA: Centers for Disease Control & Prevention; 2018.

(21) Guttmacher Institute. U.S. rates of pregnancy, birth and abortion among adolescents and young adults continue to decline. New York; 2018. Report No.: September 7, 2017.

(22) National Vital Statistics. *Births: Final data for 2016*. Washington, DC; January 31, 2018. Report No.: 67.

(23) Gurrentz B. *America's family and living arrangements: 2018*. Washington, DC: U.S. Census Bureau; 2018. Report No.: November 15, 2018.

(24) Bui Z, Miller C. The age that women have babies: How a gap divides America. *New York Times*, August 4, 2018.

(25) Livingston G. *Age of mothers at childbirth and age specific fertility*. Washington, DC Pew Research Center; 2018.

(26) Livingston G. The changing profile of unmarried parents. Washington, DC: Pew Research Center; April 25, 2018:1–5.

(27) Newport F. Americans greatly overestimate percent gays or lesbians in U.S. *Social and Policy Issues* May 21, 2015:1–5.

(28) Rasmussen Staff. *Presidential election hurts personal relationships*. Asbury, NJ: Rasmussen Polling Company; 2018.

Chapter 4

Mother's Impact on Father-Daughter Problems

"When I'm upset with dad, I get mom to talk to him for me. What's wrong with that?"

"My daughter won't talk to me when she's upset without going to her mom first. That hurts."

"Mom would be crushed if I did things with dad without including her. Can you blame her?"

"When I want time alone with my daughter, it's like I'm intruding on the mother-daughter thing."

"It's just natural for a daughter to be closer to her mom than to her dad because they're both women."

"Mom would be jealous if I went to dad with personal things instead of going to her."

"I feel like my wife's sidekick. She says she knows more about how to raise a girl than I do."

Do these comments sound familiar? Probably so, because in most families, daughters are generally closer and talk more with their mothers than with their fathers. And in many families, dad does feel like mom's sidekick who is pushed aside in the parenting. This is not to say that most daughters love their mothers more than they love their fathers. Sadly, though, throughout their lifetimes, most mothers and daughters get to know one another better and talk more about personal things than do most fathers and daughters. Even when the daughter loves both parents equally, she generally turns to her mother more often for advice on personal matters, confides more in her, and communicates more often and more comfortably with her.[1]

In and of itself, mother-daughter closeness may not seem like a problem. But as we will see in this chapter, certain aspects of that closeness can contribute to tensions and complications between the father and daughter. How does this happen? What do mothers say or do that makes it more difficult for fathers and daughters to get the most out of their relationship? How do even the most loving, well-meaning mothers sometimes limit or damage the father-daughter bond?

To be clear, very few mothers intentionally or knowingly set out to weaken or to complicate their daughter's connection to her father. Indeed, most mothers are not aware that certain behaviors and attitudes are having this negative impact. Nevertheless, the fact remains: even the most loving mother sometimes contributes to the difficulties between father and daughter. Given this, fathers and daughters need to understand how the difficulties between them might be related to the mother's behavior or beliefs.

★ Step 1: Consider the Research

As explained in earlier chapters, the first step is to consider the research. The goal in presenting this research is not to demean mothers. The goal is to help us recognize how mothers inadvertently and unknowingly sometimes contribute to the troubles between fathers and daughters. The first step is for the father, the daughter and the mother to become familiar with the research in these next four sections: idealizing mothers, father-friendly mothering, gatekeeping, and enmeshment and role reversals.

Idealizing Mothers and Motherhood

Fathers and daughters start out with a disadvantage in part because our society idealizes mothers in ways that undermine the father-daughter bond. Media, commercials, children's storybooks, TV sitcoms, and films generally portray mothers in more favorable ways. Compared with dads, moms are more unselfish, understanding, sympathetic, insightful, trustworthy, and self-sacrificing. Even Father's Day cards often make dad look like a moron compared to mom. Indeed, you will have a hard time finding Mother's Day cards that make women look as incompetent and insensitive as fathers. American children and their parents are surrounded by messages that idealize mothers and that sideline, denigrate, or mock fathers. In contrast to mothers, fathers are often presented as childlike and dimwitted when it comes to parenting, especially when it comes to parenting a daughter or a young child. In case you think anti-father advertising is not a serious issue, think again. In Britain and in several other European countries, it is against the law for advertisers to portray fathers in demeaning, sexist ways; for example, by creating an ad where the dad does not know how to change a diaper.[2]

Another way society idealizes mothers is by exaggerating the differences between men and women in ways that favor women and demean men. According to a large body of research, men are not less empathic,[3] less sympathetic and nurturing,[4] or less cooperative than women.[5] Nor are men more self-centered or more insensitive to other people's feelings than women.[6] These negative and false portrayals of men work against fathers and daughters in the same way that negative and false portrayals work against any group of people. These false beliefs set the daughter up to expect the worst from her father and the best from her mother. And those expectations affect how she relates to each of her parents.

The point is that idealizing mothers is not beneficial for fathers and daughters, particularly when it comes to being able to discuss and resolve the tensions between them. Idealizing mothers makes it less likely that the daughter will turn to her father for advice and comfort. Expecting that he will not respond as well as her idealized mother, the daughter is also less likely to go to her dad when they have issues. Instead, she tends to go behind his back to talk to her mother. This prevents the father and daughter from learning how to communicate honestly and comfortably with each other. It also creates a situation where the father often feels hurt, ignored, and helpless.

Idealizing someone also makes it more likely that we will blame others for any mistakes that our idol makes. We deny reality and lie to ourselves about who that person really is. We are blinded to reality by the shiny halo we have put over that person's head. We get angry and defensive if anyone points out our idol's flaws—even if that person is a therapist. We cannot bare to think about the things that our idol has done wrong. We push those thoughts out of our minds or create excuses for our idol's bad behavior. When remembering the past, we remember mainly the good and seldom the bad things about our idealized person.

How does idealizing mothers or motherhood complicate the father-daughter connection? First, you are more likely to side with your mom against your dad. You see your dad through her eyes, not through your eyes. You are more likely to blame dad for things that are not his fault and to let mom off the hook. You are prone to see your dad in a much more negative light than you see your mom. You are more likely to see your dad's imperfections and mistakes in ways that drive a wedge between you. You may be overly critical of him in part because you are trying to preserve your image of your mother as the saint, the martyr, or the fragile victim. You might also refuse to see how she is contributing to the troubles with your dad.

When we are very young, we idealize both parents. This makes us feel safe and secure which is a good thing. But as we age, our parents need to make sure we stop idealizing them. We need to see our

What Do You Think?

Quiz 9: Idealizing Mothers and Motherhood

What do you believe is true for most Americans today?

1 Most women choose jobs that demand less time than most men's jobs.
2 Some mothers do not want their husbands to do any more of the childcare.
3 Most fathers earn nearly 70% of the family's income.
4 When both parents have full-time jobs, fathers still work seven more hours a week than mothers.
5 Most fathers wish they could spend more time with their children.
6 Mothers are generally more sensitive, compassionate and cooperative than fathers.
7 Women have an inborn instinct for mothering and nurturing children that men lack.
8 Fathers are far more likely than mothers to physically abuse or kill their children.
9 Almost 30% of American daughters are sexually abused by their biological fathers.
10 Mothers have a greater impact on children than do fathers.
11 Mothers are far more stressed than fathers trying to balance work and family.
12 Mothers enjoy being parents far more than fathers do.
13 When children reach school age, mothers spend about three times more time with them than fathers do.
14 Compared to women, men say being parent is less important to their happiness and identity.
15 The main reason mothers do more of the childcare is that dads refuse to do it.

_____ Your Score

parents realistically as lovable, but imperfect, people. Dad needs to let his daughter know that he is not a Prince Charming or Superman. Dad needs to allow his daughter to see that he is sometimes weak, confused, frightened, fragile, and vulnerable, just like her mother. And mom needs to make certain that the children do not put her on a pedestal or view her as the superior parent.

Use the following "What Do You Think?" quiz to see how your beliefs about mothers and fathers compare to the realities. Do you have an idealized image of mothers and motherhood? Are your beliefs about fathers in line with the facts? Are you idealizing mothers and making negative assumptions about fathers based on society's stereotypes and false beliefs?

Which of the statements in the quiz did you think were true? The correct answer is: the first five. The remaining 10 are false. Here are the facts:

- Even though more women than men graduate from high school and college, most women still choose jobs that require shorter hours and have more flexible schedules than men's jobs.[7,8]
- Some mothers want to do almost all of the childcare and feel threatened when the father does too much.[9,10]
- Until all the children are in school, dads earn two-thirds of the income and moms do two-thirds of the childcare.[11]
- Even when women have full-time jobs, most men have to work longer hours, work more night shifts, and commute longer distances.[7]
- Regardless of their educational level, most fathers wish they could spend more time with their children and less time at work.[12,13]
- There are no significant differences between men and women in regard to being compassionate, sympathetic, cooperative, or concerned about personal relationships.[5]
- There is no maternal instinct in humans.[14]
- Mothers are more likely than fathers to abuse or kill children under the age of four.[15]
- Fewer than 2% of daughters are sexually abused by their biological father.[16]
- The father's impact on children is as great as the mother's and is sometimes greater in areas such as academic achievement and behavior.[17]
- Fathers are as stressed as mothers trying to balance family and work.[11,18]
- Fathers say they enjoy spending time with their children slightly more often than mothers do.[19,20]

- Mothers with full-time jobs spend about 30 minutes more a day with their school-aged children than fathers do.[21]
- Men and women are equally likely to say being a parent is important to their identity.[11]
- The main reason fathers do not spend more time with their children is because men have to work longer hours, work more night shifts, and have less flexible schedules than women, even when women have full-time jobs.[21,22]

Father-Friendly Mothers

Fathers and daughters will also have an easier time working through their issues together when the mother has always been father-friendly. By father-friendly, I mean that, from the time the children are born, the mother's beliefs and her behavior work for, rather than against, the children creating as strong a bond with their dad as they have with her.

From the time the kids are born, the father-friendly mom actively and enthusiastically shares the parenting. She allows and encourages the father to be equally involved in the children's lives. She does not constantly criticize or supervise his parenting. The father-friendly mother is not rolling her eyes, arching her eyebrows or making disapproving faces that let the kids know she thinks their dad is incompetent—an unwanted intruder and a rookie player on *her* parenting field. When she disapproves of his parenting, she lets him know in private, not in front of the children. She does not act as if she is the child-rearing expert and dad is her inferior sidekick or her slow-witted student. In short, she shows the children that she believes their father is just as good a parent as she is.

The father-friendly mother disciplines the children without turning their dad into the "bad cop." For example, when the children misbehave and the dad is not home, she disciplines them on her own. She does not shirk her responsibility and throw the burden onto the dad: "Just wait until your father gets home!" She confidently stands up to the children and exerts her authority without making the dad do all the dirty work as disciplinarian. The father-friendly mother is strengthening the children's bond with their dad by not allowing the kids to see her as the nurturing parent and him as the disciplinarian. And she does not align herself with the kids against their father. For example, she does not undermine the dad by saying: "Let's not let your father find out what you did because he will get mad at you. I won't tell him what you did. It will just be our little secret." She also lets the children know that their dad is doing just as much as she is to contribute to their happiness and well-being. She does not give children the impression that she sacrifices more or understands them better than their dad does. She builds the dad's confidence as a parent and encourages him to be *equally* involved in their children's lives. And she does not lead her daughter to believe that the mother-daughter bond is more special or more unique than the bond with the father.

Unless the mother makes it clear to the children that their dad is contributing as much as she is, children can easily get the idea that their dad—or all dads—do less for them than their moms do. In part this happens because a lot of the childcare work that men do is invisible to children. Children do not see the many things their dads do on their behalf: repairing, assembling, installing, cleaning and maintaining things, doing yard work, shoveling snow, cleaning gutters, moving furniture, repairing the roof, doing the book-keeping and financial planning (health and car insurance, taxes, investments), replacing heat and air conditioning filters, cleaning basements and attics, building fires, unplugging drains. In contrast, the mother's contributions are more visible: cooking, cleaning, washing clothes, shopping, taking kids to the doctor and driving them around. Kids are much more likely to appreciate and thank mom: "Thanks, mom, for the great dinner," than they are to thank dad: "Great tax return and super clean gutters. Thanks, Dad!"

The father-friendly mom is not jealous of the time the children spend with their dad. She does not compete with him for the children's time or attention. Here is a simple test to see how jealous or competitive your mom might or might not be. How would your mother feel if you phoned and asked to talk to your dad, without her being on the phone? Would she be okay with this as long as you were only talking to him about impersonal things like sports, money, or school stuff—but not okay if you were talking to him about your boyfriend or your husband, trouble with a female friend, or feeling depressed? Here is another test. How would your mom feel if you and your dad went out for a meal together from time to time without her—or if your dad visited you and your husband without taking mom along? Does your mom want to have these private conversations and private times with you, but feel uncomfortable about you and your dad doing the same? If so, why? Is she jealous? Insecure? Competitive?

Responding to these two hypothetical situations, many real-life daughters acknowledge that their mothers are jealous, insecure, and competitive.

> "If I asked to talk to dad on the phone, my mom would automatically think I wanted to talk about money. She'd be really hurt

when she found out it was something personal. She'd feel replaced and her self worth would be diminished."

"No way! My mother loves the position she holds—the one who has to know everything that's going on in the family. She always has to be on the phone or in the room."

"When Dad and I are trying to talk, Mom literally talks over him like he didn't exist. I can't get as close to him as I want because it would reinforce her insecurity about not having a career."

"Mom would die if I ever talked to Dad about my boyfriend instead of talking to her. She would never say anything directly to me, but she'd let me know I had hurt her. I have never shared much with Dad because I don't want to hurt Mom."

"I couldn't do it because Mom has always wanted me to feel closer to her and to need her the most."

"Now that Mom is working two days a week, my dad takes off from work early so we can spend time alone talking on the phone without upsetting her. But that's as far as we can go."

"When I tell her that Dad and I are getting closer, I get the feeling she thinks my relationship with him is just fine the way it is. I don't think she'd like my spending a weekend alone with him."

"You've got to be kidding! My mom is already jealous just because I'm taking your Fathers and Daughters course. If Dad and I did those things, she'd find some way to make us feel guilty."

"When I was a teenager, Dad always took my brother off on fishing trips and I was so jealous. When I would complain to Mom, she'd say that it wouldn't look right for my dad and me to go away together for a weekend now that I was a young woman. In retrospect, I don't think she should have had that attitude."

As one dad explains:

"Even when Jessica was a little girl, my wife got jealous when she thought I was intruding on her mother-daughter thing. She just wasn't comfortable when Jess wanted to do things alone with me. She'd get very competitive, like we were in some kind of contest for Jess's love. When Jessica became a teenager, my wife came right out and told me that 'it doesn't look right to people' for me and Jess to go off camping together the way we always had. So I backed off. I didn't want my wife upset with me all the time."

Generally speaking, father-friendly mothers have several things in common.[23] They had a joyful, loving bond with their father while they were growing up. These women value and appreciate men as parents, instead of looking down on men or feeling that fathers are not as necessary as mothers. These moms usually work outside the home even when their children are young. They are less likely than stay-at-home moms to become overly possessive of the children in ways that can weaken the father-child connection.

Use the "Father-Friendly Moms" quiz to take a closer look at how the mother in your family felt and behaved while the children were growing up. The higher the mother's score on this quiz, the easier it is for dads and daughters to create a close bond, communicate well, and work through their issues together.

Father-Friendly Moms Quiz

How father-friendly were Mom's beliefs while the children were growing up?

0=never, rarely; 1=most of the time; 2=almost always

____ Your father is just as loving and nurturing as I am.

____ I want you to talk to dad about personal things just like you talk to me.

____ Your dad has sacrificed as much as I have for you kids.

____ You and your dad need to be just as close as you and I are.

____ Your dad understands you as well as I do.

____ Your father is just as sympathetic and kind-hearted as I am.

____ You and your dad need to spend just as much time alone with each other as you and I do.

____ You ought to have private conversations with your dad without me around.

____ You and your dad need to work out your problems together instead of going through me.

____ Your father enjoys being a parent as much as I do.

____ Score out of 20

Enmeshment and Role Reversals

Besides father-friendly mothering, the mother enhances the father-daughter bond when she does not become enmeshed or reverse roles with her daughter. When the parents' marriage is an unhappy one, mothers are more likely to turn to one of their children for comfort, advice, and emotional support. Usually they turn to their daughters instead of their sons. Carried to the extreme, in her search for comfort and advice, the mother can become enmeshed or reverse roles with her daughter—a situation that is extremely damaging for fathers and daughters.

Enmeshment is an unhealthy, damaging situation where two people become overly involved in one another's lives in ways that destroy their individual identities.[24] There is no longer "me" and "you" with our own individual thoughts, feelings, and separate identities. There is only "we." "We" have to embrace the same thoughts, feelings, and decisions—especially how "we" feel about Dad. Although any two people can become enmeshed, enmeshment usually occurs between a mother and one of the children—usually the daughter. When this happens, the daughter becomes her mother's confidante, protector, defender, and advisor. It is as if the daughter has reversed roles with her mother, becoming her mom's parent and caregiver. The mother pulls the daughter into the middle of the parents' conflicts, sharing negative information that widens the gap between father and daughter. Mother and daughter become more like best friends or sisters than like parent and child—aligned together against Dad. Understandably, the daughter slowly withdraws from her father emotionally, and he, feeling rejected and unwanted, slowly withdraws from her.

Enmeshment takes a toll on dads and daughters. As a daughter, you absorb whatever negative beliefs and feelings your mother has about your father. You treat him like she does—belittling or criticizing him, ignoring or avoiding him, demeaning or nagging at him. Because you feel responsible for making mom happy, you feel you have to stand up for her and take her side. You are caught smack in the middle of her troubles with your dad. No matter how old you are, you might feel guilty about moving too far away from her because she needs you so much. And if you try to pull away from her, she makes you feel that you are being selfish or unkind. The higher a daughter's score on the enmeshment quiz, the more likely it is that the ties with her father will grow weaker.

Are Mother and Daughter Enmeshed in Your Family?

In your family, how enmeshed were the mother and daughter?

0=never, 1=rarely, 2=fairly often, 3=almost always

The daughter . . .

____ has a hard time saying no to her mother.
____ feels it is her responsibility to make mom happy.
____ has a hard time being happy when mom is unhappy.
____ feels it is her job to help mom solve problems in her life.
____ feels selfish or guilty when focusing on herself instead of on mom.
____ puts her own needs aside in order to make mom happy.
____ feels like mom's counselor, advisor or best friend.
____ worries excessively about her mother.
____ feels guilty if she disagrees with mom
____ feels like a parent to her mother

____ Your Score (30 possible)

The Mother's Negative Impact: Reflections by Real Daughters

"Mom has always told me that women have a special intuition that men don't have. But I think what's really going on is that she'd be hurt if I was really close to dad."

"My mom is constantly putting my dad down for small things she doesn't like about him. So I have also taken on a nagging tone with him. I know he hates the way we talk to him like he's a child. I've got to stop doing this."

"Mom tells me about their fights. This puts me in the middle. When they're fighting, she asks me to go to dinner with her. Once she actually turned the car around and drove us back home because I refused to listen to her complain about my dad."

"Mom points out his flaws in front of me. It makes me and my father uncomfortable around each other."

"I wish mom would stop telling me about their fights. But when I tell her I don't want to hear it, she says I don't care about her. She says I am taking his side when I tell her to leave me out of their crap."

"The hostile things she tells me about Dad stick in my mind for much longer than a few hours. I take to heart everything she says and find myself resenting my dad."

"My mom doesn't have many friends. She has always told me and my sister about her arguments with dad. She's even asked us if we think she should leave him. It makes it very difficult to see him from my own perspective."

Gatekeeping and Hoarding the Parenting

How well fathers and daughters deal with whatever is going on between them also depends on whether the mother has opened or closed the parenting gate. In most families, mothers are the gatekeepers who determine how involved the father is allowed to be in the children's lives. As the gatekeeper, she can either open or close the metaphorical gate between the father and the children. The more she opens the gate, the stronger the children's ties can become with their dad. When mothers close the gate, they are hoarding the parenting rather than sharing it with the father. It is also worth noting, by the way, that gay and lesbian couples also engage in gatekeeping in raising their children.[25]

Psychologists have developed the "Gatekeeping Scale" to assess how willing mothers are to share the parenting and encourage strong bonds between the children and their father.[10] For example, a gate-closing mother tends to supervise, correct, or criticize the father's parenting. She may also complain to other people and to the children about his weaknesses as a father. She hoards most of the parenting for herself. She is the decision-maker and the judge when it comes to the father's role. The more the mother closes the gate, the more the father becomes discouraged and withdraws from the children. In contrast, the gate-opening mom treats the dad like an equal partner, not like a sidekick. Not surprisingly, gate-closing, enmeshment, and role reversals all are more common when the parents are not happily married and the mother turns to one of her children for emotional support.

Mothers who are the most likely to open the parenting gate and allow fathers to be equal co-parents generally have several things in common.[5] These mothers generally had loving, supportive relationships with their fathers while they were growing up. They grew up in families where fathers and mothers were equally important and equally valued. They realize that, although men and women sometimes relate differently to their children, a mother's ways of parenting are not superior to a father's. In contrast, the gate-closers more often grew up in single-parent, divorced, or unhappily married families. They did not have a close, joyful, meaningful connection to their father. In these ways, the quality of a mother's relationship with her own father spills over into the next generation of fathers and daughters.

Gatekeeping

Was Mom a Gate "Closer" in Your Family?[5]

How often did mom engage in these behaviors in your family?

0=rarely, 1=occasionally, 2=often, 3=almost always

Control

____ Make him do what you want him to do with the child
____ Monitor his time with the child
____ Impose your will on him
____ Keep him from making parenting decisions
____ Set the rules for how he parents the child
____ Supervise his interactions with the child

____ Your score (18 = highest gatekeeping)

Encouragement

____ Say positive things about how he talks/interacts with the child
____ Compliment him about his parenting
____ Ask his opinion about parenting
____ Say positive things like "you're good with the children"
____ Support him in completing a parenting task
____ Tell the child positive things about him

____ Your score (18 = lowest gatekeeping)

Discouragement

____ Tell other people what you dislike about his parenting
____ Not cooperate with him on parenting tasks
____ Criticize him as a father
____ Roll your eyes at him when he talks/interacts with child to show your frustration

___ Tell the child what you think the father did wrong
___ Pretend to support his parenting decisions
___ Say sarcastic comments when he interacts with the child
___ Attempt to undermine his parenting decisions

___ Your score (24 = highest gatekeeping)

★ Step 2: Don't Make Assumptions

In the second step, the daughter explores her father's feelings and experiences as a parent. Was he pushed out or invited in?

Who Is This Man?

Quiz 8: Fathering: Pushed Out or Invited In?

While the kids were growing up, or even now . . .

1 Did you feel your role as a father was just important as mom's role? Why?
2 Were there ever times mom or anyone else made you feel like a second-class parent or like nothing more than her side-kick? What was that like?
3 Did you ever feel that TV shows or movies or commercials made men look stupid as parents? How did that make you feel?
4 Did you ever feel left out of the parenting loop and wish you had been allowed to be more involved in your children's lives? How do you wish it had been different?
5 Do you feel we kids treated you the same way we treated mom in terms of coming to you for advice or letting you know what was going on in our lives?
7 Do you feel our society values fathers as much as it values mothers? Why?
8 Did you ever feel pushed aside or devalued as a parent compared to mom? When?
9 Were there times you felt my relationship with mom got in the way, or limited or ever damaged my relationship with you?
10 Did you ever feel mom was too close or too involved with us kids? If so, what did you do about it?

The Superficial, Awkward Father-Daughter Relationship

As we just saw from the research and quizzes, mothers have a profound impact on the kind of relationship fathers are allowed or encouraged to create with their daughters. If the mother has had a negative impact, the father and daughter will often wind up with a relatively superficial and somewhat uncomfortable relationship. They rarely talk about personal or meaningful things. They almost never spend one-on-one time together without the mother around. Communication is awkward, difficult, and sometimes very strained. Instead of communicating with each other, they communicate through the mother. Most of what they know about one another on any personal level comes largely from the mother. The dad and daughter are not openly hostile to each other and rarely argue. In fact, the daughter has more arguments and conflict with her mom than with her dad. But this is not because she and her dad get along so well or have such a close bond. The reason they rarely fight is because they have such a shallow relationship—cordial and calm, but shallow.

The dad is more like an uncle than a parent. He plays a part in his daughter's life, but nowhere near the part her mother plays. Like an uncle, he is physically present without having much presence in his daughter's thoughts. Uncle Dad is not someone she feels comfortable sharing personal information with, turning to for advice on personal matters, or talking to about meaningful topics. Like an uncle, dad keeps a certain emotional distance from his daughter as well. They get along okay. But in many ways, they are strangers.

As we just saw from the research, this usually occurs when the mother or the daughter idealize mothers and motherhood, or the mom has been closing the parenting gate or has become enmeshed and reversed roles with her daughter. A combination of these factors is a recipe for demoting a father to an uncle.

The dilemma facing these fathers and daughters is how to create a more meaningful bond. How do they move beyond the superficial? How do they get to know one another at a deeper level? How do they learn to spend time together without the mother having to be there as the communicator, facilitator, and mediator? How does the dad become more than an uncle?

Alicia, her father, Herb, and her mom, Helen, exemplify this disconnect between father and daughter. She and her dad get along fairly well, but she does not feel very close or emotionally connected to him. As she puts it: "We don't talk about personal things. We just stick to the surface stuff like movies or sports. After I started high school, he lost interest in me. He stepped back and let me and mom do our mother-daughter thing. That's just natural I guess." In contrast, she says about her mother: "We've been each other's best friend since I was in high school. We talk or text almost every day, even when one of us is on a vacation. She has always said she wouldn't know what to do without me. Last year I turned down a promotion because it would have meant moving to the other coast. Since I plan to have kids someday, I'm not going to move far from Mom since I'll be depending on her even more than ever."

Herb sees the situation a little differently. He agrees that Alicia has been much closer to her mom than to him since she was a teenager. But, unlike Alicia, he does not feel that he lost interest or voluntarily stepped back. He feels he was booted out, largely by his wife, but also by his daughter. "Around the time Alicia started her period, Helen didn't seem to want me to be as involved as a dad. She kept reminding me that I couldn't understand Alicia the way she could because I'm not a woman. I guess I just got tired of arguing with her over things like going off alone with Alicia the way we did when she was younger—hiking or even running errands together. Alicia didn't seem to want me around much anymore. I felt like an intruder. I still do. But why fight it?"

★ Steps 1 and 2

The first step is for Alicia and her dad to consider the research that is presented in this chapter. The second step is for Alicia to set aside plenty of time with her dad to explore the "Who Is This Man?" questions. These two steps will help them see how they got to where they are now. This does not mean they should blame Helen for the awkwardness or distance between them. It simply means they need to recognize that what Helen says and does has held them back from becoming closer and more comfortable with each other.

★   **Step 3: Identify and Share Your Fears**

Herb's fears are about losing even more ground with his daughter. He knows the two of them aren't very close, but at least things are relatively calm between them. His fear is that, if he is honest with Alicia and tells her that he feels rejected and unwanted, she might react badly. He wants to tell her that he would like them to be closer. But he's afraid she will either get angry or distance herself further from him. Instead of a calm, shallow relationship, they might end up with a stormy, shallow one. On the other hand, as he ages, he feels even sadder about the emotional distance between them. Thinking more about old age nowadays, he feels it might be worth the risk to share his feelings with her. He's also thinking that, since Alicia hasn't lived at home for years now, it might be easier to spend time with her without Helen being around—or maybe without Helen knowing. Then again, he's afraid Alicia will tell him that she doesn't want to be closer. Does he want to take that chance?

Herb also has a second set of fears—his wife's reactions if he tries to get closer to Alicia. He already knows she enjoys being Alicia's "main" parent and best friend. If he starts stepping in, instead of continuing to step back, he fears Helen will punish him somehow. She might distance herself from him emotionally. She might badmouth him to Alicia or work harder to intensify the mother-daughter bond and to marginalize him. When grandchildren eventually come along, she might become even more competitive with him for Alicia's attention.

Alicia has some of the same fears as her father. If she and her dad worked at becoming closer, she fears her mom's reactions. Will Mom put her on a guilt trip? When there are grandchildren someday, will Mom refuse to help out? Alicia also fears that things might not get better with Dad, even if they both try. If that happens, then she has created a mess with her mom with nothing to show for it. Why bother? Why risk it? On the other hand, she has to admit that at times she has envied how other women and their dads get along—how they turn to him for advice, how comfortable they are with him, how well they know each other.

★   **Step 4: Propose a Plan**

Let's assume the best outcome: Alicia and her dad both decide they are willing to take the risk of upsetting Helen. They have shared their feelings and fears with each other. Now they have to come up with a way to resolve this two-pronged dilemma: How to create a more meaningful bond and how to deal with Helen's reactions.

Both Alicia and her dad decide to set some time aside each week to talk on the phone and to meet once every couple of weeks for coffee. This small step will probably be awkward since they are not used to talking one-on-one or spending time alone with each other. Since the goal is to move beyond talking about superficial things, they need some kind of structure to help things get moving in the right direction. They decide to use the questions in the "Who Is This Man?" quizzes in the previous chapters as conversation starters. But instead of focusing only on Herb's answers to the questions, Alicia will also answer them. This will create a more natural conversation and be less of an interview. The goal is to get to know one another better through one-on-one conversations without anyone else around.

They also decide to try getting more comfortable with each other by sharing a few activities that they both enjoy—especially light-hearted activities that might get them laughing together. They both enjoy going to religious services, art museums, and movies. So they make a plan to do one of these activities each month. On a lighter side, they agree to email or text something funny to each other every week—a joke, or cartoon, or funny YouTube—anything that might make the other person laugh. To get more focused on the closer bond they had when Alicia was young, they spend several hours looking at old photograph albums and talking about their good times together. After taking these initial steps together, Herb suggests they go on a day trip to the neighborhood where he grew up. He wants to show her around, including a visit to the cemetery where his parents are buried. Alicia is initially hesitant, but she agrees to go. Hopefully, as time passes, these kinds of activities will draw them closer. Regardless of how things eventually turn out, any improvement is better than the "uncle" relationship they have now.

The bigger hurdle is probably going to be dealing with Helen. Based on the past, they realize that she is probably going to feel jealous, rejected, and perhaps angry. In their own ways and in their own words, Alicia and Herb have to get these messages across to her: You're a wonderful mother. Unfortunately, over the years, as father and daughter, we have spent too little one-on-one time with each other. So that is what we have decided to do from here on. What better gift can a mom give her daughter and her husband than to help them get closer?

What Alicia and Herb have to make clear to Helen is that they *are* going to be spending time together without her, whether she approves or not. At the same time, they need to reassure her that this is not going to weaken the mother-daughter connection. To make the transition easier, Alicia and Herb initially arrange most of their phone conversations, texting or emailing at times when Helen is not around. They often talk when they are both still at work, where they have privacy and do not have to worry about Helen feeling left out. Whenever they spend time together without Helen, they are careful not say things that would make her feel insecure or jealous. Their goal is to help her redefine "good" mothering—to see that the most loving and best moms help fathers and daughters build stronger bonds, no matter how late in life that process begins.

Equal Opportunity Daughters

Understanding the mother's influence helps us figure out ways to strengthen father-daughter bonds in our families. This understanding helps us change those beliefs and behaviors that limit or damage the connection between a daughter and her dad. Although there are many factors that contribute to superficial, uncomfortable father-daughter relationships, the mother is generally part of the picture. Acknowledging the role that mothers and societal beliefs play, fathers and daughters have a better chance to create a closer, more comfortable connection in the remaining years of their lives.

Still, daughters themselves play a role in determining how much impact their mothers have on their father-daughter relationships. In that light, daughters should ask themselves how good a job they have done over the years giving their fathers an equal opportunity to build strong bonds with each other. And if you haven't been an equal opportunity daughter, it's time to start.

Are You an "Equal Opportunity" Daughter?

Have you given your dad an equal opportunity to get to know you and for you to get to know him?

0 = never, very unequal; 1 = rarely, unequal; 2 = usually,
    fairly equal; 3 = almost always, completely equal

____ I tell him just as much about what's going on in my life.
____ I invite him to do things alone with me.
____ I ask him personal or meaningful questions.

____ I ask him about his childhood.

____ I ask what's going on in his life besides his work.

____ I ask him to do errands or just hang out with me.

____ I talk with him about my feelings.

____ I ask him for advice on personal matters (not money, school, or work).

____ I phone, text, or email him without involving mom.

____ I talk with him about our past together.

____ I talk to him directly about problems between us.

____ I act interested and appreciative when he asks about my life.

____ I put equal thought into the gifts I buy for each parent.

____ I tell him I love and value him.

____ I spend just as much one-on-one time alone with Dad.

____ Your score (45 possible)

Reference List

(1) Nielsen L. *Fathers and daughters: Contemporary research and issues.* New York: Routledge, second edition; 2019.

(2) Siegel R. Women who can't park cars, men who can't change diapers: Britain bans ads depicting harmful gender stereotypes. *Washington Post,* June 17, 2019.

(3) Eisenberg N, Lennon R. Sex differences in empathy. *Psychological Bulletin* 1983;94:100–131.

(4) Barnett N, Rivers C. *Same difference: How gender myths hurt our relationships.* New York: Basic Books; 2004.

(5) Balliet D, Li N, Macfarlan S, Van Vugt M. Sex differences in cooperation: A meta-analytic review of social dilemmas. *Psychological Bulletin* 2011;137:881–909.

(6) Walker L. Gender and morality. In: Killen M, Smetana J, editors. *Handbook of moral development.* Mahway, NJ: Erlbaum; 2006. 93–115.

(7) B.L.S. *Time spent in primary activities by married mothers and fathers by employment status: 2007–2010.* Washington, DC: Bureau of Labor Statistics; 2015.

(8) Cha Y, Weeden K. Overwork and the slow convergence in gender gap in wages. *American Sociological Review* 2014;79:457–484.

(9) Jia R, Schopppe-Sullivan S. Relations between coparenting and father involvement in families with preschool-age children. *Developmental Psychology* 2011;47:106–118.

(10) Puhlman D, Pasley K. The maternal gatekeeping scale. *Family Relations* 2017;66:824–838.

(11) Parker K, Livingston G. *Seven facts about American dads.* Washington, DC: Pew Research Center; 2017.

(12) Bianchi S, Robinson J, Milkie M. *Changing rythyms of the American family.* New York: Sage; 2006.

(13) Livington G. Dads say they spend too little time with their children. Washington, DC: Pew Research Center; 2018. Report No.: January 8.

(14) Hrdy S. *Mothers and others: The evolutionary origins of mutual understanding.* Cambridge, MA: Belknap Press; 2009.

(15) Oberman M, Meyer C. *When mothers kill.* New York: New York University; 2008.

(16) Finkelhor D. *Childhood victimization:Violence, crime and abuse in the lives of young people.* New York: Oxford University Press; 2014.

(17) Lamb M. *The role of the father in child development.* New York: Wiley; 2010.

(18) Patten E. How parents balance work and family life when both work. Washington, DC: Pew Research Center; 2015. Report No.: November 4.

(19) Connelly R, Kimmel J. If you're happy and you know it: How do mothers and fathers in the U.S. really feel about caring for thie children. *Feminist Economics* 2015;21:1–34.

(20) Musick K, Meier A, Flood S. How parents fare: Mothers' and fathers' subjective well-being in time with children. *American Sociological Review* 2016;81:1069–1095.

(21) Bianchi S, Sayer L, Milkie M, Robinson J. Housework: Who did or does or will do it and how much does it matter? *Social Forces* 2012;91:55–61.

(22) Harrington B, Fraone J, Lee J, Levey L. *The new millenial dad: Understanding the paradox of today's fathers.* Boston, MA: Boston College Center for Work & Family; 2016.

(23) Schoppe-Sullivan S, Altenburger L, Lee M, Bower D. Who are the gatekeepers? Predictors of maternal gatekeeping. *Parenting Scientific Practices* 2015; 15:166–186.

(24) Titelman P. *Differentiation of self: Bowen family systems theory perspectives.* New York: Routledge; 2015.

(25) Sweeney K, Goldberg A, Garcia R. Not a mom thing: Predictors of gatekeeping in same sex and heterosexual parent families. *Journal of Family Psychology* 2017;31:521–531.

Chapter 5

Divorce and Dad's Remarriage

"My daughter has pushed me away ever since the divorce. No matter how hard I try, she's not very interested in being with me. I feel like her mother is turning her against me. Even though I've paid all my child support, my daughter thinks I'm stingy and selfish. I feel there's nothing left to do but leave her alone. She treats me like her mom was the only one who raised her. Why can't she see how much I've been hurt?"

"Things have been strained with Dad. I think he cares more about his girlfriend than about me. I get the feeling I don't matter that much anymore. Besides that, I worry when I'm with him that he might say something bad about mom—or that he'll want to talk about their divorce."

"After the divorce, things just sort of fell apart between us as time passed. I'm not even sure why exactly. Now it just seems like there's no way to reconnect. I don't even know what the first step would be—or which of us should make the first move. It's been so long."

"My daughter lived with me for five years because she and her mom didn't get along. But when she turned 16, she said she wanted to go live with her mother—just see me every other weekend. I was in shock. Of course I didn't force her to keep living with me. But she seems to grow more and more distant. Sometimes she's actually hateful towards me. When I ask what's wrong, she says 'nothing.' Is there a point where I should stop seeing her until she starts treating me better?"

Do the real-life situations of these fathers and daughters sound familiar? After parents separate, most father-daughter relationships undergo turmoil that weakens and complicates their bond. Sadly, the damage can be so severe that the relationship ends altogether. In this chapter we will explore ways to fix some of the most common problems that come between fathers and daughters after the parents separate. In that light, it's worth noting that only 55% of American daughters spend their entire childhood living in the same home with their father.[1] A little under half of all daughters have parents who are separated. Roughly 40% of all children are born to unmarried parents, most of whom separate well before the child's fifth birthday. And 40% of married parents eventually divorce. In short, parental separation affects a huge number of father-daughter relationships.

American Families[1]

Who Are Children Living With?

51%	married mother and father
4%	unmarried mother and father
11%	single mother, never married
12%	single mother, divorced
14%	mother and stepfather
5%	neither parent
2%	mother and her boyfriend
1%	single father, never married
1%	single father, divorced
1%	father and stepmother
0.5%	father and his girlfriend

★ **Step 1: Consider the Research**

Let's start by examining the research and assessing your beliefs. This research can be divided into two broad categories: the mother's influence and society's beliefs.

The Mother's Influence

It might surprise you to learn that divorce usually damages the father's relationship with his daughter more than it damages the relationship with his son.[2] Understanding why can help you figure out what weakened your bond and how you might repair it.

First, in the years before the separation, the daughter is usually closer to her mom than to her dad and the two of them share more personal information with each other. This does not mean the daughter loves her mom more than her dad. But it does mean, compared to the dad, the mother and daughter spend much more time together, talk about more personal issues, and share more details about what is going on in their lives. Unfortunately, this pattern means that the daughter is more likely than the son to hear bad things about her dad from her mom after the parents separate.

Second, as discussed in the last chapter, mothers are more likely to be enmeshed and to reverse roles with their daughters than with their sons. Both of these situations weaken the father-daughter bond and are more likely to happen when the parents are not happily married. Long before the parents separate, these mothers and daughters are already aligned with one another against the dad. When the daughter is already her mom's confidant, advisor and help-mate, the parents' separation widens the gap between her and her dad.

Gatekeeping Checklist

How often does or how often did the mother in your family engage in these gatekeeping behaviors? The higher the score, the greater the damage to father-daughter relationships.

0 = never, 1 = occasionally, 2 = often

___1   Asking children to keep secrets from their dad
___2   Making fun of gifts that dad gives the children
___3   Using the children as messengers to communicate with dad
___4   Refusing to allow pictures of the dad in the children's rooms
___5   Not delivering messages from dad to the kids
___6   Not sharing important information about the children with the dad
___7   Changing the children's last names
___8   Not putting dad's name or contact information on school or medical records
___9   Bad-mouthing dad, his parents or his wife
__10   Giving children access to information that might damage their relationship with dad
__11   Arguing with dad in front of the kids
__12   Not having children ready when dad comes to pick them up
__13   Telling children her financial problems are dad's fault
__14   Not following the parenting time schedule
__15   Eavesdropping on children's calls or emails with dad
__16   Putting children in the middle of parents' arguments
__17   Scheduling children's events during dad's time
__18   Not letting dad know about children's upcoming events or appointments
__19   Making contact difficult with dad's extended family
__20   Discussing child support issues with children

____ Your score (40 possible)

Many mothers make extraordinary efforts to maintain and strengthen their daughter's bond with her father after the parents separate. Sadly, there are fathers who turn their backs on their children no matter how hard the mothers try to keep them engaged. Not surprisingly, these are the fathers whose bonds with the children were not strong even while the parents were together. Many loving, dedicated fathers, however, feel they are pushed out their children's lives by the mother. As we discussed in the last chapter, mothers sometimes close the parenting gate which creates distance between the dad and his kids—especially his daughter. After parents separate, the mother's power to control the parenting gate skyrockets because 85% of children live with the mother, seeing their father only every other weekend or less.

After the breakup, the mother can close the fathering gate not only by what she says to the children, but by how she behaves.[3] Many of her behaviors are subtle. Others are glaringly obvious. Using the Gatekeeping Checklist, think back to how the mother in your family behaved after the separation. How much of a gate-opener or gate-closer was she? Even now, what does she say or do to open or close the fathering gate?

Society's Influence:
Negative Stereotypes and False Beliefs

Mothers play a powerful role in shaping the kind of relationship the father will be able to create with his daughter. But society's negative stereotypes and false beliefs about divorced fathers also have a big impact. As discussed in earlier chapters, we are surrounded by negative beliefs and demeaning stereotypes about fathers. This is especially true when it comes to divorced fathers. Many television shows, movies, and media encourage us to assume the worst about divorced dads. The typical divorced dad is presented as a childish, self-centered, irresponsible blockhead. Often, he dumps his devoted wife and abandons his kids for a much younger, beautiful woman. While mom is struggling to make ends meet, dad is having the time of his life. Child support? Forget that. Dad is spending all his money on himself and his girlfriend. So let's start with the "What Do You Think?" quiz about divorced dads. How many of the statements do you believe are true about the majority of divorced parents in the U.S.?

What Do You Think?

Quiz 10: Divorced Parents

What do you think is generally true in America today?

_____ Most states' custody laws give fathers the right to have as much parenting time as mothers have.

_____ Most divorces happen because the husband physically abused his wife.

_____ Fathers and mothers are treated equally in custody laws.

_____ Fathers generally lose interest in their children after a divorce.

_____ Financially most fathers are far better off than mothers after divorce.

_____ Mothers are usually more depressed than fathers after their divorce.

_____ College-educated mothers are rarely angry about money after divorce.

_____ The husband is usually the one who files for the divorce.

_____ Most divorced fathers do not make their child support payments.

_____ Most mothers want the fathers to have half of the parenting time after divorce.

_____ Your Score

What was your score? Hopefully, zero. Not one of the statements is true, as you can see from the research presented here. Not surprisingly, the more of these beliefs children hold when their parents separate, the more likely they are to end up with a damaged relationship with their dad. Remember: the negative beliefs that we have about any group of people influences how we treat them—even when our beliefs are dead wrong. This is why it is important to ask yourself: what did your family members believe about divorced dads before the parents broke up?

- In the largest federally funded study ever conducted, fathers were left with only $25 a month more than mothers.[4]
- Eighty percent of divorced fathers pay their full child support.[5]
- Many mothers do not want the father to have more than every other weekend time with their children.[6]

- Kentucky is the only state with a custody law that gives fathers half of the parenting time.[7]
- Fathers are more depressed, stressed, and suicidal than mothers after divorce, mainly because they miss their children.[8]
- Most states' custody laws give mothers far more parenting time than fathers.
- College-educated mothers are not less angry about financial matters than other mothers after divorce.[9]

Some of the most damaging false beliefs have to do with adultery. Although adultery is not the main reason why most parents separate, if the daughter assumes, or if she knows for sure her dad cheated, this can destroy their bond. The catch is that the daughter might be jumping to the wrong conclusions about her dad. And she is more likely to make this mistake if she already holds negative beliefs about men and cheating. So take a minute to compare your beliefs about adultery to the facts. How many of the statements do you believe are true in the "Who Cheats?" quiz?

What Do You Think?

Quiz 11: Who Cheats?

What do you believe is true about most Americans today?

1 Between the ages of 29 and 49, men and women are almost equally likely to cheat.
2 Between the ages of 18 and 29, women are somewhat more likely than men to cheat.
3 After the age of 50, people are much less likely to cheat than when they were younger.
4 Adult children are more likely to cheat than adults in their parents' generation.
5 The main reason most couples divorce is that the man cheated.
6 College-educated people are far less likely to cheat than less-educated people.
7 When both spouses work, cheating is more likely than when the wife is a homemaker.
8 In almost half of all marriages, at least one spouse cheats.
9 Religious people are far less likely to cheat than less religious people.
10 Cheating is far more common now than at any point in our nation's history.

_____ Your score

How accurate are your beliefs about adultery? Only the first two statements are true. The rest are false.[10] Let's take a closer look at some of these surprising facts. Between the ages of 18 and 29, women are slightly more likely than men are to cheat—11% vs. 10%. Between 29 and 49, women are only slightly less likely to cheat—13% vs. 16%. The largest difference between men and women is for people in their 60s. At this age, 16% of women and 24% of men cheat. Religious and college-educated adults are not more faithful than less educated, less religious adults. But cheating is more likely when the husband is the only wage earner and the wife earns no income than when they both have jobs. Still, cheating is no more or no less common than it was 30 years ago. As for the causes of divorce, cheating is not at the top of the list. Most couples say they broke up because one or both of them felt their emotional needs were no longer being met, or because financial issues and poor communication tore them apart. Adultery is a factor; but it is not the major one and not more likely for men than for women between the ages of 18 and 60.

What is the take-home message for you, as fathers and daughters, from all of this research? What should you both keep in mind as you try to resolve your particular divorce-related problem? First, whatever changes took place in your father-daughter relationship depended in part on several factors beyond your control: the mother's attitudes and behavior, society's negative beliefs about fathers, and our nation's child custody policies. Second, fathers, mothers, stepmothers, and daughters might all make mistakes that contribute to the stress and the damage to the father-daughter bond.

We have taken the first step in the four-step approach by considering the research. So now let's apply the next three steps.

Money: The Ongoing Battle

Not surprisingly, money is often at the root of the turmoil between fathers and daughters after the parents separate. We can see how financial issues have been driving a wedge between Angela and her dad, John, ever since her parents separated 10 years ago when she was in high school.

Over the years, Angela has felt resentful because her dad ended up with a higher standard of living than her mother. Although her parents started out on an equal financial footing when they divorced, over time her dad has been able to create a much nicer lifestyle than her mom. Not only does he earn far more money than her mom, who never remarried, he is married to a woman with a good income and an impressive career. During her college years, the gap between Angela and John grew larger because he refused to pay for 100% of her education and living expenses. He paid most of it. But he could easily have afforded to pay all of it. Instead, he insisted that Angela and her mother chip in as well.

As Angela puts it, "Dad makes plenty of money. So why didn't he help mom out more when my brother and I were living with her when we were in high school? He could have given her even more money so we could have lived in a house as nice as his. He and his wife take lots of vacations and shop at the most expensive stores. But mom worries about money all the time. It's hard on her because she knows how well-off dad and his wife are. Who knows how much money he spends on his wife—or how much she's going to inherit when he dies. Dad could be a lot more generous with me and my brother. We both have big credit card debts and school loans. He's just so stingy."

John definitely does not share Angela's view. Since Angela's mom did not work while they were married, he had to pay for virtually all of the children's expenses in the years after the divorce. He also had to give her half of his retirement account and half of all the assets they accumulated during their 14-year marriage On top of that, he had to pay three years of spousal support so his ex-wife could get additional training in order to get a job. He still gets upset when he thinks about all of those financial losses. Worse yet, he was not the one who wanted the divorce. Yet he was the one who, in his mind, got ripped off financially. He feels he was more than generous paying as much as he did for both children's college educations.

As John explains, "Sure, I had the money to pay all of her college education. But she and her mom needed to assume part of that burden. I'm tired of getting treated like a banking machine by the women. My son doesn't treat me that way. Besides it's not my fault her mom didn't want to work while we were married. That was her choice. It's also not my fault that my current wife makes such a good income. If my ex had remarried, she'd be in much better shape financially. But that's not my fault either. I feel like Angela is blackmailing me in a way. She keeps making little comments that if family members *really* care about each other, they help each other out financially. I'm not dumb. I get the picture. It's like money laundering. She wants me to pay off her debts so she will have enough money to help her mom out. It's like under the table alimony. Angela just doesn't appreciate all I have done for her. I hardly get a thank you. But every time her mom spends a dime on her, Angela goes all gaga."

Sadly, John and Angela share many of the same negative feelings about each other. Both are holding onto anger about money issues from years ago. Both feel mistreated and, to a certain degree, unloved. Both feel that the other is being selfish, greedy, and materialistic. Both also realize that the mom's financial situation adds to the stress between them. When we unpack this situation, we can see that there are three underlying concerns contributing to the tension. First, how much of John's money are his children and his wife entitled to—not legally entitled, but entitled in terms of keeping family ties strong? Second, how do John and Angela define love in terms of what each of them feels a father should give his children financially after they become adults? Third, what part should a stepmother play in resolving these kinds of financial issues between her husband and his daughter?

★ Step 2: Don't Make Assumptions

After John and Angela have taken the "What Do You Think?" quizzes at the beginning of this chapter, they will know enough about the research to recognize which factors contributed to their troubles. They are now ready for the second step. Angela needs to find out what her father thinks and believes on the issues. More importantly, she needs to find out why he holds those beliefs. All of the "Who Is This Man?" questions in Chapter Three are about money. So that is where she should start in order to get a general overview of her dad's feelings about a wide range of financial issues. Once she has that general information about his beliefs, she is ready to take the more difficult step: asking her dad the following questions that are specifically related to her parents' divorce.

Step 3: Identify and Share Your Fears

John's fears are pretty apparent. He fears that if he and Angela talk about the financial issues that have created stress between them for years, she will withdraw more from him emotionally and spend less time with him. She might badmouth him to her brother. He is also afraid she might create tension between him and his wife by making hurtful comments to the two of them about how well-off they are compared to her mom. His wife has already scolded him for not doing enough to get Angela off their backs about the money gap between her parents.

Angela's fears are a little difficult to pinpoint at first. But after some honest soul-searching, she has to admit that she is afraid of getting

Who Is This Man?

Quiz 9: Financial Issues After Divorce

1   When you and mom separated, how were the marital assets divided? How did you feel about that at the time? And now?

2   How were your child support payments determined? How did you feel about that at the time and now?

3   What do you wish had been different about the financial arrangements between you and mom while you were married?

4   What do you wish you had done differently when it came to financial stuff when you two separated?

5   How do you feel about prenuptial contracts? Why?

6   What do you feel a father's financial obligations should be to his children after they finish their educations? Does his being remarried affect that in any way?

7   When it comes to inheritance, what do you consider fair in terms of what a remarried father leaves to his biological children, his stepchildren and his wife?

8   What role should a stepmother play in financial decisions that her husband makes about giving money to his children?

stuck with having to help her mom financially, especially after she retires. If her dad would pitch in now by giving Angela more financial help, then she would have more money later on to help her mom. Her other fear is easier to spot. She fears that her stepmother is getting too much of dad's money—both while he is alive and after he dies. But she fears that if she admits this to her dad, it will make her look like a free-loading mooch. Frankly, she is also afraid that he might leave her even less money in his will, or be even less willing to help her financially, if she comes across as greedy and selfish.

★   Step 4: Propose a Plan

In retrospect, John realizes that he made several mistakes with Angela. First, given how little additional money was involved and how much resentment his daughter still feels, he wishes he had paid for all of her college education. What it cost him in emotional losses with his daughter was not worth what it would have cost him in financial losses.

Second, he realizes that he should not have chronically complained to Angela about all the money he had to pay her mother. He let his anger at his ex-wife spill over into his relationship with his daughter. He also has to admit to himself that he was trying to punish his ex-wife by constantly griping to Angela about the money. Deep down, he was hoping Angela might feel closer to him if she saw him as the one who had been mistreated in the divorce. It backfired. His venting only ramped up the turmoil with his daughter with no gain for him. He was going to have to pay the money and give up half his assets no matter how much he grumbled about it. Venting to friends would have been harmless. But venting to his daughter gave his ex-wife a gift. It drove his daughter closer to her mom and further from him.

Third, John blundered by not talking to both of his adult children about the financial arrangements that he and his wife made when they got married. As it turns out, in his will he has equally divided everything between his wife and his two kids. A third for each of them. He also should have explained to his children, *before* he remarried, that he is not supporting his new wife the way he supported their mother throughout their marriage. With her own income, his wife pays half of all the household expenses and the mortgage and pays for all her personal expenses like clothes, car, and vacations with her female friends. At the time he remarried, his children were old enough to have been comfortable with these discussions about money.

When he and Angela sit down to discuss a plan, he owns up to his mistakes. He makes no excuses. He fesses up. He apologizes. He explains the financial arrangements in his current marriage, including the details of his will. At the same time, he explains in detailed terms what Angela and her brother can and cannot expect from him financially from here forward. She is disappointed to learn that both of them are on their own in terms of getting any more financial help from Dad. Barring some catastrophic event in adult children's lives, her dad does not believe parents should continue to prop their kids up financially as adults. During their conversations, he explains why he feels this way. But here is the more important message he conveys to her: his decisions on these financial matters are *his* decisions based on *his* values. He reassures her that he is not being swayed or manipulated or hoodwinked by his wife.

For her part, Angela has some fessing up to do too. She admits to her dad that she has been wrong in expecting him to help her financially so she can then help her mom. Angela and her brother need to work out a plan together for helping their mom out later in life. She also agrees that she needs to stop complaining to her dad about "poor" mom and all the things "mom can't afford to do like you can." The reality is that her mother is not poor. Yes, she has a much lower income and much less money saved for retirement than dad and his wife. But Mom has been able to maintain a middle-class lifestyle and that is not likely to change after she retires.

Hopefully, with both of them making these changes, Angela and John can reduce the stress over financial issues that has been hanging over them for years.

Dad Remarries: Wicked Stepmoms

Of course, money is not the only source of stress between fathers and daughters when a stepmom comes along. As the following "What Do You Think?" quiz shows, daughters are far more likely than sons to have a difficult time getting along with their stepmothers. Compared to sons, daughters are more rejecting, more critical, and more competitive with their dad's wife. Generally, the troubles between the two women stem from three sources: jealousy, insecurity, and unrealistic expectations about blended families.

Mark, his daughter, Robin, and his wife, Anne, are in over their heads on all three counts. Even though Robin and her brother were in their 20s when their dad remarried, things have not gone well on the father-daughter front. His wife has one son from her first marriage. But since he lives on the other side of the country and is in his late 30s, he has had virtually no impact on the remarried family dynamics. In contrast, the tensions between Mark's daughter and his wife were apparent to everyone from the time he and Anne got engaged. Although she and her brother came to the wedding, it was clear that Robin was not thrilled about being there. Anne and Robin are cordial enough. But they both make petty, snide remarks about each other to Mark. At family gatherings, the two women tend to avoid each other as much as possible or just chit chat about superficial things. When Mark is with the two of them, the two women are clearly not at ease and neither is Mark. Mark feels caught in the middle of the two women he loves.

Mark often feels discouraged, hurt, and worried. "My daughter and wife take their frustrations with each other out on me. I'm trying to be a good husband and create a real family here. I'm no spring chicken.

This marriage has to work out. The two women are cordial enough, but it's tense and awkward and a little phony. I'm always making suggestions to each of them about what they could do to become real friends. That always backfires. This isn't what I expected and hoped for. It's been two years since Anne and I got married. But we're still not a family. It's gotten to the point that I spend less and less time with my daughter and her family. Recently she really made a mess of things by refusing to address Anne as Grandma in a thank you card to the two of us from my grandson. Things are just going downhill with the two women I love most."

Robin sees things differently. "After Dad met Anne, he pretty much lost interest in me, my son, and my husband. He's always talking about Anne. He brags about her like she's a little kid. He dotes on her. He tries to make me feel guilty for not becoming friends with her. Dad and I used to enjoy spending one-on-one time together. That never happens anymore. Now everything has to be a family event with Anne there. She's always around, even when I'm talking to Dad on the phone. And Dad has meltdowns whenever I do the slightest little thing that hurts her feelings. The most recent breakdown was over a thank you card I sent them from my four-year-old son for a birthday gift. I addressed the card to 'Grandpa and Anne.' No wonder I'm always walking on eggshells around them."

Of course, Anne has her own perspective and feelings about all of this. She feels that no matter what she does, she can't please Mark or his daughter. "The harder I try to get close to her, the more she pulls back. I'm always bending over backwards trying to win her over. Even after two years, she still treats me like an outsider who is intruding on *her* family. At Thanksgiving she brought videos over for all of us to watch together—videos of her and her brother growing up, with her mom and dad smiling away. I was so uncomfortable that I excused myself to go clean up the kitchen. I know I shouldn't have, but I got really mad at Mark after everyone left. It's a little awkward too when she introduces me to people as 'my dad's wife' instead of 'my stepmom.' What bothers me most is that this is taking a toll on my marriage. Mark is so focused on how she feels that he's losing his focus on us."

★ Step 1: Consider the Research

In this situation, considering the research is especially important. Mark has very unrealistic expectations that are increasing the stress on everyone. The two women feel pressured to live up to his expectations because they both love him. But none of them realize that very few blended families function the way Mark believes they do. Learning about this research can help all three of them come to grips with the reality of how most blended families work. This knowledge is key to becoming more relaxed with one another.

Which of the statements in the following blended family quiz do you believe are true? If you are in a blended family, which of those beliefs do other members of your family hold? Which of those beliefs creates or used to create tension in your family?

What Do You Think?

Quiz 12: Blended Families

What do you believe is true for most Americans today?

_____1   Most sons and daughters are more accepting of stepfathers than of stepmothers.

_____2   The stepmother-stepdaughter relationship is the most difficult relationship in most blended families.

_____3   When their widowed dad remarries, daughters are far angrier than sons at their dad and at his new wife.

_____4   Most children, even as adults, are more upset than when their dad remarries than when their mom remarries.

_____5   Fathers and stepfathers generally get along better than mothers and stepmothers.

_____6   In blended families, even adult children want to spend some time alone with their parents.

_____7   More than half of Americans are or will eventually become part of a blended family.

_____8   Second marriages are more likely to end in divorce than first marriages.

_____9   Stepparents have no legal custody rights in terms of being allowed to see their stepchildren if the marriage to the children's biological parent ends in divorce.

_____10 Most fathers get remarried to women 10–15 years younger than they are.

_____11 When a dad remarries in midlife or very late in life, the blended family rarely has problems.

_____12 Stepmothers generally get along better than stepfathers do with their stepkids.

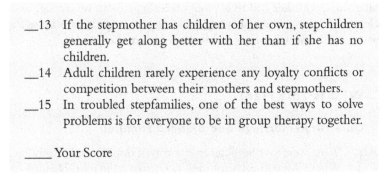

___13   If the stepmother has children of her own, stepchildren generally get along better with her than if she has no children.

___14   Adult children rarely experience any loyalty conflicts or competition between their mothers and stepmothers.

___15   In troubled stepfamilies, one of the best ways to solve problems is for everyone to be in group therapy together.

_____ Your Score

Which statements did you think were true? Statements 1–9 are true and statements 10–15 are false.[11,12,13,14,15] The most difficult relationship in blended families is usually between the father's daughter and his wife. But even the son has more trouble accepting a stepmother than accepting a stepfather. Why? In part because dad usually remarries before mom does. So the stepmom is the first stepparent that the children have to get used to. Then too, when dad remarries before mom does, the children often feel sorry for their mom if she is not in a relationship. Feeling sorry for their mom makes it more likely that the kids will feel disloyal or guilty if they like their stepmom. A stepdad also has two other advantages over the stepmom. His income raises the mom's standard of living and his biological children only spend every other weekend, if that, with him. This means the kids have to cope with stepsiblings far more often when their dad remarries than when their mom remarries. Another bonus for stepdads is that dads and stepdads generally get along better than moms and stepmoms. In short, the stepmom usually gets the short end of the stick. In terms of dealing with stepfamily strife, the worst idea is bringing the entire family together for group therapy. Instead, the parent and stepparent should work privately with a therapist to create solutions as a couple, before involving any other family members in any kind of therapy.[14]

★ Step 2: Don't Make Assumptions

After becoming familiar with the research, Robin and her dad and stepmom should all have a much more realistic picture of what they should aim for as a blended family. Still, Robin should take plenty of time alone with her dad to explore his feelings about remarriage and blended families. The following questions can help them both get a better handle on what fears and feelings each of them have.

Who Is This Man?

Quiz 10: Remarriage and Blended Families

1   What were you hoping for in terms of our blended family?
2   Where did you get your ideas about what the ideal blended family should be—movies or TV shows? Blended families you know personally?
3   How should blended families be different from intact families?
4   What does your wife think is the hardest part of being a stepparent?
5   What do you wish you had known and done differently before you remarried?
6   What are some of the things you worry most about in our blended family?
7   If you could change just three things about our blended family, what would they be?
8   How have your beliefs or feelings about blended families changed over time?
9   What advice would you give to each member of our blended family?

★   Step 3: Identify and Share Your Fears

Everyone's fears are fairly obvious in this family. The daughter fears losing Dad to the stepmom. The stepmom fears losing her husband. And the dad fears losing the closeness he so desperately wants with the two women he loves. Jealousy and insecurity have the upper hand here. On top of that, everyone is unsettled trying to live up to some imaginary fantasy of how a blended family is supposed to function.

Robin feels jealous and insecure because her dad is now less attentive to her, her son, and her husband. She fears that the family ties are deteriorating because her dad is too focused on his wife. Her measure of how little her dad cares about her and her family is based on two things: his spending less time with them and his spending no time alone with her since he got married. To her, Dad's love is like a pie with six slices that he hands out based on how much he loves each person—five pieces for his wife, one piece for his son, and one measly piece for his daughter to share with her son and her husband. She's also irritated with her dad because he talks so much about his wife and talks so little about her son, the only grandchild.

Then there are Anne's feelings and fears. Her main fear is that, down the road, all of this mess could cause her marriage to collapse. This is a second marriage for her and for Mark. She knows from experience that things can go downhill fast even in the best marriages. She is also frightened because she is in the one-down position. She is the outsider in the family that Mark has with his two children, his grandson and his son-in-law. That family also includes his ex-wife, because she is actively involved with their grandson, the daughter, and the son-in-law. In contrast, Anne only has one son, no grandchildren, and no daughter-in-law. And her ex-husband is not a part of any family system. So the family that Anne has to interact with the most is Mark's family, not hers.

Then there is Mark, caught between the two women he loves. He shares Anne's fears about the long-term impact this mess might have on their marriage. He also has fears about the impact on his connections to his daughter and his grandson and, though to a lesser extent, his son-in-law. Could things reach a tipping point where all of these family ties are permanently damaged?

His heart is in the right place. But he is clueless when it comes to seeing how he is contributing to this mess. His biggest mistake is that he keeps pushing the women to measure up to his unrealistic image of a blended family. This makes both women feel they are failing him, and it ramps up the tension between them. He is out of touch with reality when it comes to how most blended family members feel about each other and how they interact. He is also ignoring the reality that neither his wife nor his daughter feel any need to become friends. Both women are perfectly fine relating to each other in a cordial, yet superficial, way.

Mark is also fueling Robin's bonfire of jealousy and insecurity. His first mistake was spending so much less time with her and her family after he met Anne. His second error was talking too much about Anne in his campaign to get Robin to like her. When Mark married Anne, Robin was a new mother with a young baby—Mark's only grandchild. Even though he had just married Anne, this was the worst time for Mark to cut back on his time with his only grandchild and his daughter and son-in-law. Finally, he is making his wife feel insecure by focusing so much on how she relates to his daughter. It is definitely time to make changes.

Robin and Mark take the third step by sharing their fears with each other. In this situation, Mark and Anne also have to sit down together and share their fears. Once everyone's fears are out in the open, it's time for the final step.

★ Step 4: Propose a Plan

Mark takes the initiative to ask Robin to get together and talk about a plan. He takes the first step in proposing a plan because he realizes that he is the one who has contributed the most to everyone's stress. Once he absorbs what the research shows about blended-family realities, he realizes that he has to change his expectations for his wife and for his daughter. In the "Who Is This Man?" conversation with his daughter, they both realize where his unrealistic ideas came from and where they need to change. Now he takes the fourth step by explaining to his wife and to his daughter what specific changes he is going to make. He has these conversations with them separately.

In talking to his daughter, he admits that he was wrong in trying to pressure her to become friends with his wife. He also admits that he should have carved out more time alone with her and her family. They take out their calendars and choose several dates to get together over the next two months. He also admits that he has been making too big a deal about little things, like her not introducing people to Anne as a stepmom. "After all, it's not like she helped raise you. I can see why you feel more comfortable introducing her as my wife than as your stepmom. It's up to you two women to decide what kind of relationship you want with each other. I need to butt out. If you eventually become friends, that's good. But if you don't, that's fine too. From here on, I'm focusing on spending more time alone with you."

But this is a two-way street. Anne needs to make some changes too. In fact, Mark asks her to refer to Anne by some nickname acknowledging that she is one the grandparents. "Your son is going to grow up with Anne in his life. So it would mean a lot to me if you'd let Anne have some kind of nickname even if it's not Grandma." He also asks her not to bring child-hood videos, family photo albums or other very personal reminders of their former family to events where Anne will be present. And he admits to her that he felt uncomfortable too when she did that.

For her part, Robin owns up to contributing to the family stress. She has been too insensitive and a little too demanding of his time in this early stage of his marriage. All married people have less time to spend with friends and family. Just because her dad and Anne are not a young married couple doesn't mean they don't have to pay special attention to the first few years of their marriage. She also realizes that she made a mistake by not telling her dad how she felt and by not taking charge of setting up time for them to be alone with each other. She tells her dad that she plans to ask Anne if she would be willing to babysit occasionally so she and her dad can go out for a leisurely dinner or for a long afternoon together. This will not only make Anne feel more welcomed, it will give her and her dad more time together. She also plans to be more aware of Anne's feelings as the outsider. Being more aware does not mean the two women have to become friends. It just means she should not ignore the fact that, regardless of how old Anne is, she still has feelings and she *is* at a disadvantage as the outsider. Robin would also be doing everyone a favor if she would spend some time talking to women who are stepmothers about their difficult, painful experiences.

Anne too, realizes she has been shooting herself in the foot. She plans to go down a different path. She tells Mark they are going to make plans for him to spend more time alone with his daughter, grandson and son-in-law on a regular basis. Everyone can benefit from this simple gift. It strengthens Mark's tie with his daughter and with his wife. This also eases things between the two women. Anne is also learning a lesson from the secret book of stepmother success: *step back*. Step back from trying so desperately to impress Robin. Step back from being included every time Mark gets together with his daughter. Step back from trying to live up to an unrealistic image of the stepmom that everyone loves. Everybody can win here if they all step back from their unrealistic expectations about blended families.

As the following comments from real stepdaughters show, the dad's remarriage can unleash a wide range of emotions, as well as leading to important insights, for their daughters.

"My mom died when I was a teenager. Fortunately my dad and I had a wonderful relationship. But now it seems to be changing. He's going to marry the woman he has been dating for a couple of years. I'm 34 now. And here is the dream I had last night: my mom, dad and I are in the living room of our old house on Birch Street. Mom says to Dad, 'Well, I'm back, just like you always wanted.' He says, 'Oh, wow. This isn't what I expected. I'm getting remarried. Can I have time to think about this?' Mom didn't answer him. But I did: 'If you choose that other woman over my mother, then I choose my mother over you!' When I woke up this morning, I realized I'm not mad at him for remarrying. I'm just missing Mom."

"When he showed me pictures of his wedding to my step-mom, I almost cried because I vividly remembered angrily refusing to accept what was happening. The picture jolted me right back to sitting pinned to a bench, helpless to prevent upheaval once again. A few days ago, I called my stepmom. We talked almost an hour—unprecedented in our relationship after 11 years. I apologized to her for many of the things she had to go through because of me."

"Currently I'm struggling with Dad just having gotten married. I feel he has his own life now and I don't feel part of it. Still, I am beginning to see the romantic side to him now that was never evident in his marriage to my mom. It makes me feel a little strange."

Reconnecting After a Long Absence

Sadly, some father-daughter relationships take such a hard hit after the parents separate that the daughter ends all contact with her dad. This break might last for months or for years. In many cases, some event eventually occurs that motivates the daughter or her father to rethink the situation and to wonder if they should reach out to one another. It might be the daughter's graduation from high school or college, or getting engaged and thinking about her future wedding, or finding out she and her husband are going to have their first child. Or it might be the father getting sick or being diagnosed with a serious illness. Should they try again after months or years of no contact?

What fears are holding them back from reaching out? First, they fear being completely rejected. The other person won't respond at all. There will be no response to emails or texts or phone messages. Nothing. Just silence. Then there is the fear of punishment. You will get a response—a punitive, angry, hateful, vicious one. There might be cursing, screaming or crying. Then what will you do? There is also the fear of not being forgiven. Will it just end up being a long, angry rehashing of the past—a painful guilt trip with no forgiveness and no way forward? Finally, there is the fear of retribution and retaliation. The retaliation might come from that person *and* from other family members. Will the person turn other family members against you after you have reached out to reconnect? For example, will an angry daughter try to turn a sibling against their dad? Or will the mother lash out against the daughter who decides to give her dad a second chance? Or will the stepmom get upset with her husband if he agrees to see the daughter who has rejected and hurt him for so long?

Giving specific advice on how to rebuild a father-daughter relationship after a long absence would not be possible without knowing why the contact ended. The advice here is simply advice on how to take the first step by reaching out—how to see if the other person is willing to have contact with you. I suggest to fathers and to daughters that you start by sending a written message either by email, text, or regular mail. Do not phone or leave a voice message. That might be too intrusive and put too much pressure on the other person. A written message gives the other person time to think. It also gives the person something tangible to re-read.

No matter how you word your written message, you want to accomplish these things. (1) Make it clear that all you want is to renew contact. You are not asking for money or for help of any kind. There is no hidden agenda. (2) Be honest about why you have been too afraid to reach out until now. What do you fear might happen? State those fears. (3) Promise that you are not going to bring any other people into this, if the two of you decide to have some kind of contact with each other. This is a private matter, just between you two. (4) Do not bring up any issues or start any discussion about what went wrong in the past. That is for much later, if you both decide you want to try to rebuild. (5) On the other hand, if you feel like apologizing for something specific that you did, go for it. Keep the apology simple and direct. (6) Include a couple of recent pictures of yourself—casual pictures doing something very ordinary, like sitting with your dog or cooking at the grill. Do *not* send pictures that might backfire on you by being misinterpreted as some kind of hurtful or mean-spirited message. For example, do not send a picture of you on an expensive vacation, or a picture with members of your new family. It's best to send a picture without other people in it.

Here is a sample letter to give you a rough idea what your written message might look like:

Dear . . .

It's taken me a long time to get up the courage to write you. Every time I've tried, I chicken out. I've been afraid that you wouldn't answer or afraid that you'd send me an angry response. I don't know exactly how to start or what to say, except that I want us to be in touch again. Nobody has put me up to writing to you. I haven't talked this over with anyone else in the family. I really just want this to be between us. There's nothing I'm asking from you—other than to have you back in my life in some way. I understand things better now about what I think went wrong between us. And I have some things I want to apologize for, if you're willing to talk to me. Could we maybe have a phone call and see how that goes? Enclosed are a couple of pictures of me from a few months ago. The goofy looking dog is a little guy I got at the pound last year. Well, I guess that's about it for now. With Care, . . .

Will It Be Worth It?

As you try to narrow the gap between you, there will be times you will feel emotionally exhausted, frustrated, angry, sad, hesitant, confused, unsettled, and maybe even guilty. You will probably wonder: will it be worth it?

Fathers and daughters experience a wide range of emotions and reactions as they work their way through the issues that have stressed their relationship after the parents' divorce or dad's remarriage. For the lucky ones, this emotional journey is one that both of them want to undertake—even though they know beforehand that it will be stressful and painful at times. Regardless of whether it is the father or the daughter who initiates the process, they both embrace this emotional voyage. For those who are not so lucky, one of them is an unwilling participant who has to be dragged along by the other. One is enthusiastically shouting "all aboard" and the other one is running lickety-split in the other direction. The runner might be the daughter. Or it might be the dad. Either way, the journey will initially be off to a rough start, since one of them is so resistant. In these situations, it's likely that the resistant one doing the running has the most emotional baggage to unpack. Still, these father-daughter journeys can be the most productive in the end.

The comments from these real fathers and daughters should give you courage to take the journey, even if it gets off to a rough start.

Their comments also remind us that, even when the outcomes fall far short of what they had hoped for, these daughters gained the peace of mind that comes from trying to rebuild the bond. Remember, too, neither of you is getting any younger. Time is running out for you to try to repair the damage caused by the breakup of your family.

> "Problems in my family are never discussed or explained—just ignored. Now 10 years after my parents' divorce, because of this talk with my dad, I learned all the missing pieces leading up to the breakup of our family. I left the conversation feeling I'd finally found someone who loves me and who had been taken away from me so many years ago."

> "Hearing him talk about the divorce was hard because he was so vulnerable. When he told me about mom falling in love with another man, I realized that he's been through what I just went through—the sinking sensation when someone leaves you. We've never had a conversation like this where we share personal stories like I do with my mom."

> "Sure, I wish my dad had treated my mom better when they were married. He was a pretty lousy husband. But that doesn't make him a lousy father. In fact, he's always been a damn good dad. I just wouldn't let him off the hook until now for being a lousy husband."

> "He actually called himself a failure regarding my sister and me. I have begun to think it was a mistake to take my stepfather's name. I now realize that this may have made my dad feel he wasn't needed. I never really thought about how he may have been hurt by that."

> "He said my contacting him was the best gift I had ever given him. I always had this vision of him as some opinionated, overbearing, stubborn tyrant. It has always been unthinkable to me that he might admit his failures."

> "I realize now that seeing mom constantly upset by him while I was growing up had a profound effect on the way I felt about him. Now I know I have to focus on my issues with him—not on hers."

> "I was really surprised that he still had wedding pictures of him and Mom. When telling me about them, he seemed to be remembering all the good times they shared. It was so nice because my mom has always given me the impression that Dad doesn't care about the life he had with us."

"The year my parents divorced my mom took me to a dog show, like my dad and I had always done. When I got there, it was just a bunch of smelly dogs walking around on leashes in exchange for liver treats from their handlers. All the magic was lost. Actually the magic was never at the dog show. The magic was my father; but he was no longer there. During my talk with him, he said one of the most meaningful things for him was going to those dog shows together. I was so happy that he remembered it the way I did."

"This long talk with my father about my parents' divorce is the most wonderful thing we have shared in over a decade. As I drove back to my apartment, I had a feeling I've never had before after seeing my father: I felt that I was *leaving* home rather than *coming* home."

"Talking to Dad helped me see that he and mom weren't ever really happy together. After they had kids, we became mom's fulfillment. Dad, feeling left out, turned to other women and alcohol. That was wrong. But at least I see now why he did it."

"One of my father's comments cut straight to my heart. When we were discussing his dreams, he said he wonders if he will ever marry again. The expressive look on his face and tone of his voice showed me how much the divorce had hurt him. I stopped feeling mad at him because I saw him as a man with a lonely heart."

Reference List

(1) Census Bureau. *Population estimates in United States*. Washington, DC: U.S. Department of Labor: Census Bureau; 2017.

(2) Nielsen L. *Fathers and daughters: Contemporary research and issues*. New York: Routledge, second edition; 2019.

(3) Austin B, Fieldstone L, Pruett M. Bench book for assessing parental gatekeeping in parenting disputes. *Journal of Child Custody* 2013;10:1–16.

(4) Braver S, O'Connell D. *Divorced dads: Shattering the myths*. New York: Putnam; 1998.

(5) Austin B, Fieldstone L, Pruett M. Bench book for assessing parental gatekeeping in parenting disputes. *Journal of Child Custody* 2013;10:1–16.

(6) Puhlman D, Pasley K. The maternal gatekeeping scale. *Family Relations* 2017;66:824–838.

(7) Hubin D. *State custody laws: 2019 report card*. Boston: National Parenting Organization; 2019.

(8) Kposowa A. Marital status and suicide in the national, longitudinal mortality study. *Journal of Epidemiology and Community Health* 2000;54:254–261.

(9) Hetherington M, Kelly J. *For better or worse: Divorce reconsidered.* New York: Norton; 2002.

(10) Fincham F, May R. Infidelity in romantic relationships. *Current Opinion in Psychology* 2017;13:70–74.

(11) Enyart S, Heisdorf S. Obstacles and opportunities experienced by adult step-children in later life stepfamilies. *Journal of Divorce and Remarriage* 2019;55:1–10.

(12) Miller C. Repartnering following divorce: Impact on fathers and their adult children. *Journal of Marriage and Family* 2013;75:697–712.

(13) Papernow P. Recoupling in mid-life and beyond: From love at last to not so fast. *Family Process* 2018;57:52–69.

(14) Papernow P. *Surviving and thriving in stepfamily relationships: What works and what doesn't.* New York: Routledge; 2013.

(15) Riches G, Dawson P. Daughters' dilemma: Girls whose widowed fathers remarry early. *Journal of Family Therapy* 2000;22:360–374.

Chapter 6

The Final Stage: Elderly Fathers

"My father was an amazing man. The older I got, the smarter he got."
Mark Twain, satirist and author, 1835–1910

"When you're young, you think your dad is Superman. Then you grow up and realize he's just a regular guy who wears a cape."
Dave Attell, comedian

Fathers and daughters can encounter difficulties between them at any age. Still, some of these stressful situations are far more likely to happen when the dad is in the latter part of his life. As his physical and mental condition declines with old age, his bond with his daughter can become unexpectedly complicated or badly damaged. Past the age of 60, a father's happiness declines more quickly than the mother's.[1] In part this might be because fathers and daughters are generally not as close as mothers and daughters. But, as we will see in this chapter, fathers' ties to their daughters are damaged by other issues as well: financial and step-family issues, the father's physical health, sibling rivalries, end-of-life care, and funeral plans.

All of the situations that we are going to explore in this chapter are related to the research on the financial and emotional costs of aging, illness, and death. So as a first step, fathers and daughters need to become familiar with the most recent research and statistics on these topics. In the following two quizzes, let's see how well-informed you are about the realities of aging, illness, and death.

What Do You Think?

Quiz 13: Aging and Dying: The Gender Gap

Which of these statements are true for most Americans today?

1 The leading causes of death for women and for men are cancer and cardiovascular disease.
2 Over the age of 70, about 15% of women and 10% of men develop Alzheimer's.
3 Two-thirds of all people with Alzheimer's are women.
4 Most men die about seven years before women do.
5 Men are more likely than women to be depressed and kill themselves after the age of 70.
6 Men are almost twice as likely as women to die from drug use or overdoses.
7 African Americans are more than twice as likely as white Americans to die of diabetes, high blood pressure, and kidney disease.
8 Men are almost three times more likely than women to die from alcoholism.
9 White men are more likely to die from alcoholism than African American or Hispanic American men.
10 The average lifespan for white men is 76, compared with 71 for African American and 79 for Hispanic American men.

_____ Your Score

Which statements did you think were true in these two quizzes? The correct answer is: all of them. All of the statements are true.[2,3,4,5,6,7] Now go back and re-read these two lists carefully. As you read them, think about the impact these realities might someday have or might already be having on your father-daughter relationship.

What Do You Think?

Quiz 14: The Cost of Aging and Dying

Which of these statements are true for most Americans today?

1 Roughly 40% of people diagnosed with cancer deplete their entire life's assets within two years.
2 The number of Americans older than 65 filing for bankruptcy has tripled from 1991 to 2018, largely because of healthcare expenses.
3 Americans are more likely than people in other advanced nations to insist on the most expensive end-of-life treatments for terminal conditions.
4 In 2015 the average yearly cost of care for the aged was $50,000 for home health, $48,000 for an assisted living facility, and $100,175 for a nursing home.
5 The average cost for a funeral in 2015 was between $9,000 and $12,000.[23]
6 About 20% of people who reach age 65 will need two years of full-time care and another 30% will need more than two years of care.
7 Nearly 8.3 million elderly people were receiving some form of paid care in 2015.
8 The number of Americans over the age of 65 will rise from 47.8 million in 2015 to 88 million by 2050.
9 Each year roughly 1.7 million people are diagnosed with cancer, with almost 90% being over the age of 55.
10 The number of people with Alzheimer's is predicted to rise from 5.7 million in 2018 to 16.1 million by 2050.

_____ Your Score

Daughters need to come to grips with the fact that, in many ways, their dads have a harder time than their moms in the last phase of their lives. After the age of 60, men are more likely than women to suffer from depression and to commit suicide.[8] In our late 60s, our happiness generally declines. But this is truer for men than for women.[9] And if the father is a widower, there are fewer sources of professional support for him than there are for the mother who is a widow. For example, men whose wives have recently died of cancer are often unable to find support groups that medical facilities make available to women whose husbands have recently died.[10]

Ironically, the most successful, most well-educated fathers often have the hardest time adjusting to and accepting what is happening in the final phase of their lives.[11,12] After retiring, many of these fathers go downhill emotionally—and they go downhill faster than fathers who were less successful in terms of income, education, or achievements at work. As the old saying goes, "the mightier they are, the harder they fall." Men who were deeply attached to being top-earning superstars are more likely to become depressed, disheartened, and difficult to deal with after they retire. These are the men who were continually striving for more and hoping to stay at the top of the ladder until the end. As these aging fathers struggle with the loss of status and income, their ties to family and friends often suffer.

The quality of the father-daughter relationship becomes especially important in his old age. When they are not close, daughters are far more likely to feel resentful and to become depressed if they end up having to take care of their elderly parent.[13] But even when they are close, daughters who have to become their father's caregiver often pay a huge financial and physical price.[14] Daughters are often forced to cut back work hours or retire early. Some daughters also have health issues of their own, including bad backs and weak knees, that make it difficult or risky to provide care for their elderly parent. Unfortunately, it is more common now than ever for people in their 60s and 70s to be taking care of their elderly parents.[15] Added to that, Americans are less likely than people in other advanced nations to follow their doctors' orders by taking their prescribed medicines.[16] This can make it especially difficult for daughters to provide care for elderly parents. This also helps explain why, even two years after their elderly parent has died, sons and daughters who were the caregivers are more likely to be clinically depressed, to have high blood pressure, and to suffer from stress-related illnesses.[17] Needless to say, these caretaking burdens are easier to live with when the daughter has a loving, close bond with her elderly dad.

Several other realities can also have an impact on the father-daughter bond. First, a father is more likely than ever before to be providing care for his elderly mother.[18] Seeing her father as a gentle, loving, caregiver might make a daughter feel even closer to him. But on the downside, daughters and sons are less likely to give emotional, physical, or financial support to their elderly fathers than to their elderly mothers.[19]

Then, too, daughters whose fathers did not help them financially after they graduated from college are less likely to help their elderly dad than daughters whose dads kept on helping them financially after they finished college.[20] Even when fathers are still in their 50s, when the father-daughter relationship is troubled, both of them are more depressed than when their bond is strong.[21]

Not surprisingly, daughters who are close to their fathers do not feel as guilty, angry, or resentful after he dies.[22,23,24] Having a close tie with her dad also helps a daughter through the grieving and healing when her mother dies in midlife.[25] In short, the quality of the father-daughter relationship can affect them both profoundly even in his old age. With all of this research in mind, let's examine several situations that can create a strain between fathers and daughters in his later years: divulging health information, dealing with financial matters including inheritance, and making end-of-life decisions including funeral planning.

Health Issues: Secrecy or Honesty?

As parents age, they almost always develop more physical health problems and become less mentally alert. Some of these health issues are minor and may hardly seem worth mentioning to their children. Yet even seemingly harmless medical procedures may unexpectedly take a turn for the worse. For example, even in relatively simple operations, an older patient can die from a reaction to the anesthesia or can have a fatal blood clot. And these risks increase dramatically as we age. A medical procedure that would pose almost no risk to a 60-year-old can pose a major risk to a 70-year-old. Given these risks, most parents let all of their children know when they have a health problem or are undergoing a medical procedure. Everything is out in the open.

But what about families where the elderly father has had little to no contact with one of his children for some time? This presents a number of complicated questions. Should the siblings or any other family members tell the estranged child what is going on? What if the sick parent objects? Do children who have cut off contact with a parent have a right to know if that parent is sick or dying? Is it fair for a parent to ask one of the children to keep this information a secret from their siblings? When a parent has a health problem, who should get to decide who in the family is told and who is kept in the dark?

These questions are more relevant for fathers than for mothers because children are far more likely to be estranged from their dad than from their mom. Especially if the parents are separated, there are sons and daughters who have had no contact with their fathers for years.[26] For example, in a national survey with more than 5,000 people ages 25 to 32, nearly 20% of them had no contact at all with their dad. In contrast, only 4% of them had no contact with their mom.[27]

All of these complications are colliding in Sue and Ellen's unhappy predicament. The two sisters are now in their 40s. Their mom died eight years ago, and their 72-year-old dad never remarried. The sisters and their dad were getting along well with each other until three years ago. For reasons that are still not clear to Ellen, her sister and her father, Ed, got into some intense wrangles with each other and eventually stopped talking. Ellen has heard both sides and still can't quite figure out what went wrong. She knows how painful this has been for her dad and her sister. But she has managed to stay out of the middle because everyone agreed years ago not to discuss the dad issue.

This "ignore it" tactic has worked well because the sisters live in separate cities and because their father does not live near either of them. Sue knows that Ellen goes home several times a year to visit their dad. This has never created tension between the sisters. At their age, they both realize that each of them has to work out their own troubles with their dad.

A few months ago, though, things changed. Ed was diagnosed with a heart condition that requires fairly complicated surgery. At 72, he is in good health otherwise, so the doctors predict a full recovery. Of course, he tells Ellen and her husband what is happening. And she has made plans to fly back home to help take care of him during the first week or so after the surgery. But here is the catch: Ed wants Ellen to promise not to tell her sister about his condition or about his upcoming surgery. And that request is damaging Ellen's bond with him. She is not only growing resentful, she is getting angry. She is angry at her dad for putting her smack in the middle of his troubles with Sue. If Sue ever discovers that Ellen has deceived and lied to her, their friendship will be damaged. And what if something goes wrong during the surgery and their dad dies? Or what if, even two years down the road, someone makes an off-handed remark to Sue that lets the cat out of the bag? All it would take is a remark like "I'm glad your dad is feeling so much better these days."

On the other hand, if she refuses to do what her father is asking, things will probably get worse between them. If she goes behind his back and tells her sister, Dad will feel betrayed if he ever finds out. She is starting to feel that her dad is being selfish and insensitive by putting her in the position of having to choose between him and her sister.

She is also angry at him because she wouldn't be in this jam if he had done more to settle things with her sister. The thought has also crossed Ellen's mind that her dad might be trying to punish Sue. Even if he is not consciously aware of it, is he figuring that if he did die from this surgery, Sue would feel really guilty for not patching things up with him? Is he trying to send her a painful message: I love your sister more than I love you? The more Ellen thinks about this, the angrier she gets. Now two father-daughter relationships are at risk.

From Ed's perspective, what he is asking Ellen to do is perfectly reasonable. Since he and Sue have not talked for several years now, why tell her about his surgery? If he told her, then she might try to reach out to him—but only because he was sick, not because she really loved him. After all, if she had truly missed him, then why hasn't she taken any steps to mend things? He is already feeling fragile and nervous about the surgery. So why add more stress by dragging Sue into it?

Ellen needs to tell her father how she feels and what she fears before things go any further. She needs to keep focused on her and her dad, not on the troubles between her dad and her sister. Here are the bottom-line messages she has to get across to him: I cannot in good conscience keep this information from my sister. If I agreed to do that, it would make me feel bad about myself and make me feel bad about you. Instead of deceiving you, I'm telling you now that if you won't tell her yourself what's going on, then I will tell her for you.

The conversation might go like this. "Dad, I'm going to be there with you the day of surgery and for a week or so after you get home. I'm with you all the way. But there is something we need to get settled before then. I understand why you don't want Sue to know about your upcoming surgery. I get it. I really do. But you're asking me to deceive my sister. And I can't do that because if she ever found out, it could ruin my friendship with her. And even if she never found out, it makes me feel bad about myself to deceive her. You're asking me to pay a price for the mess between you two. Really, Dad, how would you have felt if your mom or dad had asked you to deceive your brother about something this important? Either you need to tell Sue, or you need to let me off the hook and tell me it's okay for me to tell her."

At that point, Ellen proposes a plan to try to address her dad's fears. Her dad is afraid of having to deal with Sue's reactions to the news about his upcoming surgery. He is afraid Sue might react in ways that will stir up all the anger and hurt from the past. He's already dealing with his fears about the upcoming surgery. Ellen suggests to him that when she tells her sister what's going on, she also tells her not to contact their dad—or at least not contact him until several weeks after he gets home. Whatever Ed wants is the message that Ellen will convey to her sister on his behalf.

If Ed rejects her plan and still insists that Ellen deceive her sister, then Ellen has to listen to her conscience. She will tell her sister without letting her dad know. The possible bad fallout from deceiving her sister would be worse than the possible bad fallout from deceiving her dad.

You might think this particular situation has nothing to do with you because you can't imagine this happening your family. Think again. There are several take-home messages here for all fathers and daughters. First, a troubled or estranged relationship between an older father and one of his children can wind up having a painful impact on his other children. Second, as they age, fathers are more likely to have unexpected health crises, such as strokes or heart attacks, that leave them permanently disabled or that kill them. If there is a troubled or estranged relationship with any child, the family should talk *now* about how this is going to be handled in the future when a parent becomes ill or is dying. And third, a father should never put any of his children in the position of having to lie to or deceive their siblings. This is not only likely to create problems between the siblings—problems they did not create or deserve—but also creates problems between the father and his children.

Inheritance and Financial Decision-Making

Another source of tension between aging fathers and their children is money—an obstacle that typically has a more negative impact on daughters than on sons, as we will see. It is never too early for a parent to begin having discussions about inheritance and other financial and health matters with adult children. Unfortunately, it is often too late. When an older parent unexpectedly becomes incapacitated, too many sons and daughters find themselves in a terribly unsettling, confusing situation. Being totally in the dark about their parent's finances or end-of-life plans or wishes, even the best family friendships can be crippled, sometimes beyond repair. And when a parent dies without having put financial and end-of-life plans in place through legal documents, or without having made their children aware of their wishes, sons and daughters can wind up angry, hurt, or resentful toward one another and toward their dead parent.

Many of these financial issues are directly related to inheritance. Who is going to get what when the parents die? What will each sibling get? What will the stepmom or stepchildren get? What about the grandkids? If one child has children and the other does not, is it fair for the dad to leave part of his money to the grandkids? Or if the dad gave one child money years ago to set up a business, should the other child who received no financial help somehow be compensated in the inheritance?

Then there is the question that is generally more important for daughters than for sons because daughters do most of the caregiving for both elderly parents. Will the child who sacrificed the most in terms of taking care of mom or of dad in their old age get more of the inheritance or be repaid in any way? Keep in mind that this caregiving includes more than just the hands-on care. It includes the very time-consuming job of overseeing responsibilities for the elderly parent: talking to doctors, keeping up with financial and medical records, filing tax returns, interacting with the team of caregivers, shopping for clothes and all other items needed for the parent's daily care. This son or daughter is also the one who is on call whenever the parent needs help or just wants to talk—which often means many calls throughout the day, every day, every week. If there is little to no money to disperse after the parent dies, will this child at least be given most of the family's treasured possessions—dad's watch, mom's favorite cooking pot, great-grandpa's handmade table?

In discussing these matters, two legal terms are important—financial power of attorney (POA) and healthcare power of attorney. Financial power of attorney means the designated person (or people) is in charge of all financial decision-making. For example, the person with financial POA decides whether we can spend $5,000 a month for Dad to be in assisting living or whether the upper limit is $3,000. Healthcare power of attorney is a completely separate issue. This is the legal authority to make all decisions regarding the person's physical or mental health. For example, the person with healthcare POA decides whether Dad's memory has declined to the point that he has to be moved to a residential dementia facility. This person also decides whether the parent should be removed from life support devices when dying, if these directives are not already in the parent's will. These legal powers can be granted to anyone, not just to a family member. Wise parents will have a legal document which designates who will be in charge of making these financial and health care decisions if they became mentally or physically incapacitated or after they die.

From the perspective of preserving close family ties, the worst choice is giving health care or financial power of attorney to more than one person since this requires that both people agree. For example, if the dad gives health care power of attorney to both of his daughters, then they both have to agree on all healthcare decisions. And if they can't agree, they have to take legal action to turn the power of attorney over to a third person. Obviously, in healthcare crises, this is not a position anyone wants to be in. Likewise, if the dad grants health care power of attorney to one sister and financial power of attorney to the other sister, trouble may lie ahead. For example, the sister with healthcare POA wants to move Dad into assisted living, but the sister with financial POA wants to take the cheapest route and hire a neighbor to help take care of Dad at home.

Father-daughter ties can also be weakened by other financial and healthcare issues. Since men usually die seven years before women, most daughters will end up taking care of their widowed mother, not their widowed father. Still, while both parents are alive, the dad often plays the major role in decisions about the end-of-life financial plans. In other words, even if their father dies before their mother dies, children can feel hurt or resentful about the financial decisions their dad made. These decisions include who gets health care power of attorney and who gets financial power of attorney. And who is going to be in charge of selling the house or any remaining property after both parents die? Who will decide whether the sibling who has been living for free in the parents' rental home has to move out or has to start paying rent? And, of course, there are complications if a stepmother is in the picture.

It is extremely important to understand that family ties can be ripped apart over relatively small financial and healthcare issues. The amount of money at stake can be quite small even when the battle is big. What is at stake is not only how much each child inherits or which one gets to make the decisions for the parents. What is at stake is how loved, trusted, and valued each child feels. Even 60-year-old children can be left wondering: does my parent love me less than he loves one of my siblings, or less than he loves my stepmom? Doesn't my dad trust me as much as he trusts my sister? The family's most valuable possession might be an antique cabinet worth no more than $200. And the "big" financial decision might be nothing more than whether to move the parent's small account from one bank to another bank. But whichever child inherits that $200 cabinet or whichever child gets to make the decision about the savings account might feel more loved or more valued. Or the brother whose parents give him financial POA feels that his parents think he is more intelligent than his sister. This is how families can be torn apart even after the parents are dead.

In certain ways, the father's bond with his daughter suffers a greater blow than his bond with his son when it comes to these end-of-life matters. Why? Because the daughter usually does far more of the caregiving for her aging parents than her brother does. She is the one doing most of the emotional heavy lifting. She hopes her parents will recognize her sacrifices. She hopes they will compensate her somehow, either in their will or by paying her for some of her caregiving help over the years. She hopes her parents will see that she is the more loving child in this final stage of their lives. She hopes they will see that their other children are shirking their responsibilities. She hopes they will acknowledge that over the years they did more financially for her siblings than they did for her. She hopes they see the negative impact her caregiving has had on her health, her marriage, and her income. She hopes. In some families, her hopes materialize. But in others, her hopes are dashed and her heart is broken.

End-of-Life Directives and Funerals

In addition to financial and healthcare decision-making, there are also decisions about end-of-life care and about the funeral itself. How much medical care and what kind of interventions does the parent want at the end of life? Under what conditions does the parent want to be intubated, kept on respirators, or resuscitated if the heart stops? To what extremes does the parent want to go to be kept alive when the condition is clearly terminal? All of these directives can be included in a legal document that the person with healthcare POA must follow. If the parent does not see to it that these directives are put into a legal document, then the decisions are left up to the person or people with healthcare POA—or, worse yet, left up to no one.

Then there are matters related to the funeral itself. What does the parent want? Although it is more common nowadays for sons and daughters to have these conversations with their parents while they are both mentally and physically healthy, far too many families never discuss these issues. Some issues are strictly financial. For example, in 2015 the average cost of a traditional funeral where the body is embalmed and then buried was between $9,000 and $12,000.[28] In contrast, the average cost of cremation is about one third this. If there is not enough money left in the parent's assets to cover the funeral costs, who will pay? Should the sibling with the highest income pay the most? Should sons or daughters go into debt to pay for a parent's funeral? And how are the siblings going to make that decision when they do not all agree?

Who Is This Man?

Quiz 11: Aging and Dying

1　What worries you most about aging and dying?
2　How have your religious or spiritual beliefs changed over time?
3　What were some of your most spiritual experiences?
4　How would you like to spend the last year of your life if your health is good enough?
5　What do you hope people will remember most about you?
6　What are some of the best and worst things you experienced at a funeral or memorial service?
7　How have the illnesses or deaths of people you knew affected your feelings about sickness or dying?
8　If you could have any two spiritual questions answered, what would they be?
9　What end-of-life medical care do you want for yourself?
10　What would be the ideal funeral/memorial service for you (music, food, setting, rituals, etc.)?
11　What do you want on your tombstone, or do you even want one?
12　How do you feel about cremation and scattering ashes vs. a traditional burial?
13　Should there be a price limit on how much a family pays for a funeral? Why?
14　What do you wish had been different about your parents' deaths and their funerals?
15　Who do you want and who do you not want to be invited to your funeral? Why?
16　What would you want written about you in an obituary?
17　Do you worry that there will be tension or arguments in the family after you die? Why?
18　How do you feel about memorial services instead of funerals?
19　What do you believe about an afterlife?
20　Who do you worry most and worry least about in terms of their dealing with your death? Why?

Then there are the emotional issues. How religious should the service be? Are there rituals that will offend or upset some family members? In families where people are estranged or there is still a lot of animosity between divorced, extended, or stepfamily members, who should be invited to funeral or memorial services? Inviting Dad's older brother, weird old Uncle Joe, is one thing. But what about dad's ex-wife, the mother of his children? The children know their mom cheated on their dad, then divorced him, made off with half his assets, and treated his new wife very badly. Should mom be invited to the funeral if the stepmom does not want her there?

Unless these matters are settled ahead of time, family ties can be damaged or even permanently crippled. For the sake of the father-daughter relationship, these matters should be discussed and put to rest well before the dad's death. To prevent later heartache and distress, a daughter or a father can arrange to get together to discuss the following "Who Is This Man?" questions. This discussion can either be between the two of them or, preferably, can include all of the siblings.

Two Father-Daughter Scenarios

Let's look at the different outcomes for two sisters and their elderly father. Frank is 76 years old. His daughters' mother divorced him 35 years ago. It was a painful, humiliating, and heartbreaking ordeal because she left him for another man, after carrying on an affair for almost two years behind his back. Many years after the divorce, both of Frank's daughters learned the truth about their mother. Frank eventually remarried. His wife and he are both in relatively good health for their age. Both of them are also financially well-off enough to take care of their own needs until they die. This is why they have a legal agreement that neither of them will receive any money from the other's estate after death.

Frank has two daughters, Ruth and Margaret. Ruth is married, is still working full-time, and has no children. Margaret is divorced and retired with two married, college-educated sons and four grandchildren. For five years, she has been living for free in a modest rental house that Frank owns. Early in Margaret's career, Frank gave her a considerable amount of money to start her own business. Despite his financial help, Margaret wound up with less retirement money and a lower standard of living than Ruth and her husband. Margaret is in this position partly because she has been divorced twice and has not remarried—and partly because she made a number of costly business decisions in the years just before she retired. Even though Ruth wound up richer than her sister, Margaret is far from poor. She has ample savings and enough social security income to maintain a middle-class lifestyle until she dies. Still, she has to budget carefully, and she cannot afford the luxuries her sister enjoys. In this latter part of her life, her standard of living is definitely a big step down from what she was accustomed to for most of her adult life. In contrast, Ruth's standard of living is a big step up from what she had been used to in earlier years. In short, the sisters' financial situations have been reversed.

Because Frank's wife, his daughters' stepmother, is well-off, she and Frank signed a prenuptial agreement where neither of them would inherit money after the other's death. This means that Frank's decisions about inheritance are his and his alone. Frank has decided to leave half of his assets to each daughter—with two exceptions. He is giving Ruth an additional sum that is equal to the amount he once gave Margaret to start her business. He is also giving Ruth an additional sum that will be equal to the rent her sister has saved over the years by living for free in Frank's rental house. He leaves no money for Margaret's two grown children, because he feels that would be unfair to Ruth who has no children. His will also states that his rental house will be put up for sale immediately after he dies, and that the sale will be handled by a real estate company. This will prevent the daughters from arguing over the sale price or arguing over Margaret having to move out. He also lists specific things, like pieces of jewelry, to be given to each daughter.

To prevent future hassles between his daughters, Frank gives financial POA to an employee in the trust department at his bank. He grants healthcare POA to a young friend who works in the medical field. He has carefully spelled out the directives for end-of-life medical care—no feeding tubes, no resuscitation, no heroic measures to extend his life when he is dying. The will also contains detailed directions for the kind of funeral and burial he wants. The will explicitly states that he does not want his ex-wife invited to any of the formal or informal events at the time of his death. He has given Ruth and Margaret copies of his will so they are fully informed. Frank is pleased. Ruth is pleased. Margaret is not pleased, to put it mildly.

In this family, the two father-daughter relationships have taken a different turn—one for the better, one for the worse. Ruth feels loved, respected, and appreciated. She also happens to agree with her dad about his end-of-life decisions for health care. And she understands why her dad does not want her mother to be involved in any of his funeral services. "It means a lot to me that Dad realizes that he gave Margaret more financial help than he gave me earlier in our lives. I feel that he respects me for all my hard work and for never relying on him for money. I feel even closer to him knowing that we feel the same way about all the funeral stuff and end-of-life medical care. When I am dying, I don't want people wasting all the time and money keeping me alive another few months or weeks or days. I would have had a hard time if Dad wanted a big funeral, people looking at his dead body in a casket, and all that nonsense. I don't believe in expensive weddings or expensive funerals. Just give the money to charity in the person's honor. Scattering his ashes in a private family gathering is exactly what I want when my time comes. And given what mom did to him and how she treated my stepmom, I understand why he doesn't want her there."

Margaret, on the other hand, is angry and hurt. She feels mistreated. More importantly, she feels that her dad's decisions mean he loves Ruth more than he loves her. "Dad knows I don't have as much money as Ruth. He knows I need the inheritance money more than she does. My two sons can't help me financially because they've got young kids to raise. Besides, Ruth has a husband who can help her financially if she ever needs it. And what about my children, Dad's grandkids? Doesn't Dad love them enough to leave them something? Just goes to show that Ruth always was Dad's favorite." Margaret is also upset about her dad's end-of-life decisions. To her, cremation is "disgusting" and scattering ashes is "offensive and crude." To her, it is also morally wrong for people to refuse medical intervention at the end of their lives. But the straw that breaks the camel's back is Frank's refusing to let his ex-wife be part of any service. "Dad isn't showing much concern for me or my children. When he dies, I'm going to want my mother there for comfort. Dad's just being childish. He'll be dead. Why should he care if mom is there?"

So there we have it. If Frank had taken the opposite path, Margaret would be the happy daughter and Ruth would be the disgruntled one. But the lesson here is not whether Frank made the right decision. Maybe he did. Maybe he didn't. It all depends on a person's values or religious beliefs. The lesson here for fathers and daughters is simply this: whatever decisions a father makes about these end-of-life issues, he should be wise and loving enough to put his wishes in a legal document—or if he feels he can't afford to do that, at least to write them down and put them in a safe place. This lifts the burden from his children or other family members of having to make painful, complicated decisions while they are dealing with his dying and his death. And hopefully it will preserve the goodwill that his children have toward him and toward each other, long after he is gone.

The Final Phase

There is no way to predict how any particular father is going to deal with his physical decline, illnesses, and his impending death. What we can predict is that the way he copes with his decline will have a profound impact on his friends and family. The winding down of his life is not just a reminder that he will eventually cease to exist. The winding down process involves many losses along the way: the loss of a career identity, the loss of physical energy, the loss of a youthful appearance, the loss of mental sharpness, the loss of physical health. How can fathers and daughters keep their bond strong during this final phase of his life when so much is deteriorating?

Unfortunately, sick or dying parents do not always talk with their sons and daughters about death or dying. For example, nearly 30% of parents who were dying of cancer never discussed what they were going through with their adult children.[29] This silence was not comforting. It left the children feeling more distressed. In contrast, when older parents with cancer talked openly and honestly to adult children about their condition and about the future, everyone was more relaxed. In fact, introducing humor into these discussions was especially helpful in making every feel close and more at ease.[30]

Many adults avoid bringing up the topic of death with their terminally ill parents. Some assume that their parents will be even more depressed and frightened by their impending death if anyone brings up the topic. In fact, many terminally ill parents are not terrified of dying or overwhelmed by sadness and fear.[31] Most of us imagine that dying is always a lonely, meaningless, terrifying experience. But in a unique study with terminally ill patients, their blog posts were filled with love, peacefulness, and acceptance.[26] The closer they got to death, the more positive their blogs became. They were focused on things that helped them make meaning of life, including religion and family. This is not to say that the majority of people approaching death are going to be peaceful and positive. Still, the grim reaper may not always be as grim as we imagine it to be.

Unfortunately, for some daughters, their dad becomes more surly, distant, or mean-spirited as his health declines and his death approaches. He may feel increasingly jealous and resentful of the lives his children have. Maybe their lives are painful reminders that he never achieved what he had hoped to achieve in his own professional or personal life. Or maybe, in reflecting on his own life, he realizes that he was not the kind of father or husband he should have been. In situations like these, it is unlikely that his final years will draw him closer to his daughter.

But if a daughter is fortunate, her dad deals with the final years of his life with grace and dignity. His bond with her and with other family members deepens. He is not full of regret. He is not depressed or angry. He feels he has had a meaningful life with a loving family and cherished friends. This is the father who leaves his daughter with a comforting message: *"live your life, love your life, then let it go."*

Reference List

(1) Rauch J. *The happiness curve: Why life gets better after midlife.* New York: Green Tree; 2019.

(2) Gilligan A, Alberts D, Roe D, Skrepnek G. Death or debt? National estimates of financial toxicity in persons with newly diagnosed cancer. *American Journal of Medicine* 2018;131:1187–1199.

(3) Kochanek K. Deaths: Final data for 2017. *National Vital Statistics Reports* 2019;68:1–16.

(4) Thorne D, Lawless R, Foohey P. *Bankruptcy booms for older Americans.* Los Angelos: University of California, Consumer Bankruptcy Project; 2018.

(5) Rosenstein D, Yopp J. *The group: Seven widowed fathers reimagine life.* New York: Oxford University Press; 2018.

(6) Freedman D. The worst patients in the world. *The Atlantic,* July 2019:28–30.

(7) Harris L, et al. *Long term care providers and services in the U.S. 2015–2016.* Atlanta, GA: Centers for Disease Control and Prevention; 2019.

(8) Kochanek K. Deaths: Final data for 2017. *National Vital Statistics Reports* 2019;68:1–16.

(9) Rauch J. *The happiness curve: Why life gets better after midlife.* New York: Green Tree; 2019.

(10) Rosenstein D, Yopp J. *The group: Seven widowed fathers reimagine life.* New York: Oxford University Press; 2018.

(11) Rauch J. *The happiness curve: Why life gets better after midlife.* New York: Green Tree; 2019.

(12) Brooks A. Your professional decline is coming much sooner than you think. *The Atlantic,* July 2019.

(13) Bastawrous M. Factors that contribute to adult children caregivers' well-being: A review. *Health and Social Care in the Community* 2015;23:449–466.

(14) Boerner K, Jopp D, Kim K, Kim Y. *Very old parents and their old children: A growing and global phenomenon.* Annual Scientific Meeting of the Gerontological Society of America. Boston, MA; November 2018.

(15) Garland S. When the older care for the oldest. *New York Times,* 2019; Business, p. 5.

(16) Freedman D. The worst patients in the world. *The Atlantic,* July 2019:28–30.

(17) Coe N, Van Houtven C. Caring for mom and neglecting yourself? The health effects of caring for an elderly parent. *Health Economics* 2009;18:991–1010.

(18) Leland J. Men taking care of aging mothers. *New York Times,* November 28, 2008:A-1.

(19) Lin F. Adult children's support of frail parents. *Marriage and the Family* 2008;70:113–128.

(20) Caputo R. Adult daughters as parental caregivers. *Journal of Economic Issues* 2002;23:83–97.

(21) Polenick C, et al. Relationship quality between older fathers and middle-aged children. *Journal of Gerontology: Psychological Sciences* 2018;73:1203–1213.

(22) McMullen M. *Every fathers' daughter: 24 women writers remember their fathers.* Kingston, NY: McPherson & Co.; 2015.

(23) Secunda V. *Losing your parents, finding yourself.* New York: Random House; 2000.

(24) Mangione L, Lyons M, DiCello D. Spirituality and religion in experiences of Italian American daughters grieving their fathers. *Psychology of Religion and Spirituality* 2016;8:253–262.

(25) Cohen M, Wellisch D, Ormseth S, Yarema V. The father-daughter relationship in the wake of maternal death from breast cancer. *Palliative and Supportive Care* 2018;16:741–748.

(26) Krampe E, Newston R. Reflecting on the father: Childhood family structure and women's paternal relationships. *Journal of Family Issues* 2012;33:773–800.

(27) Hartnett C, Fingerman K. Without the ties that bind: U.S. young adults who lack active parental relationships. *Advances in Life Course Research* 2018;35:103–113.

(28) NFDA. *Funeral costs: Trends and statistics 1960–2015.* Brookfield, WI: National Funeral Directors Association; 2019.

(29) Hirooka J. End of life experiences of family caregivers of deceased patients with cancer: A nationwide survey. *Pscyho-Oncology* 2018;27:272–278.

(30) Harzold E, Sparks L. Adult child perceptions of communication and humor when the parent is diagnosed with cancer. *Qualitative Research Reports in Communication* 2006;7:67–78.

(31) Goranson A. Dying is unexpectedly positive. *Psychological Science* 2017;28:988–999.

Index

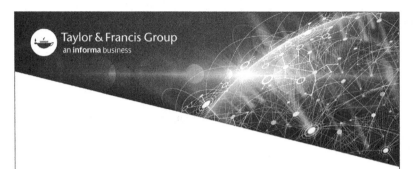

Printed in the United States
by Baker & Taylor Publisher Services